*If you have a child or know ~~spectrum you will find this book to be informative,~~ inspirational, witty and charming. Thank you Lydia for sharing your personal insights. I believe your story will help and touch many.*

- Amalia Starr, mom to adult son Brandon
  Author, *Raising Brandon*

*Lydia's book is a delightful peek into the mind of a young woman with autism. Filled with engaging scenarios from her own life, she offers insight on ways to communicate and connect, for parents who want to feel closer to their child with autism. With her sweet and conversational "voice" she encourages readers to not only help their child become all they can be, but to recognize the glory of who they already are.*

- Michelle O'Neil, mom to R, age 11
  Author, *Daughter of the Drunk at the Bar*
  Blogger, www.fullsoulahead.com

*Lydia easily puts into words both the positive and negative sides of the Autism Spectrum and gives insights to the Autism mindset. For many parents, like myself, I have often wondered what is going through my son's mind at any given moment that he is tantruming, so overjoyed that he cannot speak and only make sounds, and every feeling in between the extremes of anger and happiness. Most importantly, this entire book shows me as a parent that my son does in fact love me even though he may not verbalize or show it in a way that I am used to.*

- Emily, mom to J, age 5

*As the mother of a son with autism, I have read scores of books on the subject. Most of them are either written by parents or researchers. Lydia's book is a refreshing change because she is able to actually take the reader inside the mind of a person with autism. She also gives good advice on coping techniques for parents to use with their children. The book is well written, to the point and leaves the reader hoping that Miss Wayman comes out with another book in the near future.*

- H, mom to R, age 9

*Whilst this book is not for the feint hearted or those not acclimatized to autism it is for anyone who seeks to understand, truly understand, about living autism. Lydia pulls no punches and tells you how it really is, not how you think it might be. You will learn a lot, laugh and cry along the way and come to the end feeling enlightened, like you gained a friend. Forget theory, this is practical autism.*

- Amanda, mom to Bear, 12 and Scrumpy, 14

Revised Edition

Copyright 2011, 2014

Elsie Penelope Book Company

ISBN 978-1-257-99679-7

Living in Technicolor

An autistic's thoughts on raising a child with autism

*Revised Edition*

By Lydia Wayman

Edited by Emily I. Garland and Jennifer Kramm

# Table of Contents

Dedicated to Emily Demily

Editor,

Sister,

Friend.

# Foreword

This book will not give you a step-by-step of how-to-raise-your-child. It's not a memoir, and it won't tell you how to cure or prevent autism. What it *will* do is offer the unique perspective of one autistic young woman. It will bring you into her life, her mind, her world. It will explain how she thinks and what she believes, and it will give you her ideas about how to ensure that your child with autism is as content as he can be while still remaining autistic.

I set out to write this book because I believe there is a hole. There are books for parents and books for autistics, but where are the books written by autistics for parents of children with autism? Who better to say what works for an autistic person than an autistic person himself?

This book is a collection of short writings dated between June 2009 and July 2013. As a certified scatterbrain, I am not known for my ability to sit and write long pieces, as my attention span is not the greatest. And, I know that as a parent of a child with autism, you are not known for having long periods of time to sit and read. And so, you will find a collection of short pieces that can be taken one at a time but still form a collective whole.

The book is organized into four sections, and each section follows a similar pattern. First, there are poems I have written over the years that speak to the subject of the chapter. Then, there are a series of blog posts from my blog *Autistic Speaks* which have proven to be the most popular and helpful. Here, they are in one place and organized by topic rather than chronologically, so you may find things out of order in terms of dates. Then, I have answered some of the most common questions I get from parents, both about my life and about their children. I will say now that I cannot speak for anyone but myself... but, as a person with autism, I also have a bit of an insider's view of what makes us do what we do.

A note about the language in my book: It strikes me as odd that I, a female, would write about people with autism using the pronoun *he*. The fact is that autistic boys outnumber girls four to one, and so, it makes sense to use he. In no way do I mean to ignore the vast numbers of girls on the spectrum, but I found "he or she" rather cumbersome in writing, and so I opted for simply *he*. Secondly, it has been brought to my attention that some people object to the use of the word "autistic" as a noun. I identify both as "an autistic" and "a person with autism." I simply do not get caught up the semantic battles. In light of the fact that "person with autism" also becomes cumbersome in writing at the frequency which I would have to use it, I chose to use varied language, which includes "autistic."

As of July 2013, two years after the initial publication of this book, my life and my perspectives have changed to such a degree that I feel strongly about provided updated information. I can't address every change I've experienced, but I'd like to include snippets that show some of the ways in which I have grown (immensely) in the last two years.

**On Perspectives**

*It suddenly struck me that that tiny pea, pretty and blue, was the Earth. I put up my thumb and shut one eye, and my thumb blotted out the planet Earth. I didn't feel like a giant. I felt very, very small.*

- Neil Armstrong

## On perspective

Beneath the sun,
Beneath the skies,
Beneath a tree,
A stone there lies.

Dark and dirty,
From dusk till dawn,
There in the grass,
Upon the lawn.

Many years
Will come to pass,
Before anyone sees
The stone in the grass.

One sunny day
A human comes
It matters not who she is,
Nor what she's done.

But she steps on the stone.
And open it cracks.
Kicked to the side,
Just one half.

Now nudged into the sun,

The lonely brown stone

With brilliance casts light,

Colors,

*Brilliance.*

The world now aglow.


One inch to the left,

Or one to the right,

The sun would have missed,

The stone never shone bright.

# Me too

I talk, but I don't always speak.

I have a voice but sometimes no words.

I communicate, but I don't use nonverbals.

I laugh, but I'm not funny.

I hear, but I don't always listen.

I see, even if I'm not looking.

I write in words, even though I think in pictures.

I know, but I don't understand.

I look (sad/angry/happy/excited/scared), but maybe
I'm just the opposite.

I can answer, but only if you ask.

# I Know Why

I'm acquainted with the caged bird's song,
That which informs his melodies
His lonely fate, behind the bars,
Is just the reason that he sings.

He peers at the world outside his caste,
Watches ever from afar
For even when the door is open
He cannot live beyond those bars.

The bars aren't wrought of iron,
The door not made of stone.
But he lacks the certainty of self
He needs to stand alone.

And so he trudges on by day,
Pondering by night,
Of what his life could, or would be,
If he dared take flight.

Though he may never find within
That which he needs to fly,

He acquiesces to contentedness
In watching life pass by.

So when  the world around him beams,
He whistles songs of joy,
And when crumbles downward,
Musical tears he will employ.

But sadder yet than any song
That I've heard him impart
Is the song he whistles upon pondering
His stance of cagèd heart.

I have long been known for getting "stuck" on things.  From an interest, to an idea, to a goal, I get something in my mind and then it simply must happen.  This includes routines, or the way things are "supposed" to be.  Once I get into a routine, the world feels like it will end if that routine is disrupted.  It's a difficult thing to look past the one-track way it should be and see into the way it could be. Sometimes, all I need is a new perspective.

Autistic Speaks blog post
4 February, 2011
Alton Brown

My mind is running a mile a minute as I try to start this post. Where do I start? "Let's start at the beginning/A very good place to start." But what's the beginning?

Okay. Breathe. Do you know who Alton Brown is? If you don't, I will tell you that he is the host of *Good Eats* on the food network. Caught up now? Good.

Alton Brown is my culinary hero. He taught me how to make a beautiful omelet. He's on *every* weekend night at 11 P.M. And I stay up to watch him *every* weekend. I never miss Alton Brown. His half hour show is the most relaxed I feel all day and all night. He relaxes me as much as my cat, Elsie Penelope, does. I love Alton Brown.

He wasn't on Monday. Luckily, I was tired enough that I just went to bed without him. I was upset. I admit, I cried a tiny bit as I got panicky, but I dealt with it and went to bed and was okay by the next morning, though I hadn't forgotten. How dare Food Network deprive me of my Alton Brown? I could forgive them once. But then, last night, he wasn't on again. I had been feeling anxious throughout the evening and was desperately waiting for Alton Brown to come on. But he didn't. Really, Food Network? What's going on here?

When I saw that he wasn't going to be on, I halted mine and my friend Leigh's conversation dead in its tracks and wailed. "Alton Brown isn't on!!!!! I'm going to melt down!" I could feel it building. No answer. Leigh emailed me about some Bible verses I had asked her about earlier and I said, "Alton Brown!!!! I can't think about that when Alton Brown isn't on!" She reminded me that I could watch him on YouTube, so I did that. But that only sort of fixed the problem. He's *supposed* to be on T.V. every night at 11. Every night.

Leigh said that it was okay that he wasn't on T.V. tonight. She said that I need to think about things

I can control, not things that I can't. I asked her what I can control. She suggested that I can control what I do for a half hour every night. I thought about that. My favorite thing to do from 11-11:30 is to watch Alton Brown, but that doesn't mean that I *have* to do that. I can watch something else on T.V. or do something else altogether, like read, or write, or paint-by-numbers that I like so much. I can choose what I do every night for that half hour. My favorite thing to do is still to watch Alton Brown, but last night I chose to watch Worst Cooks in America and Facebook with Kate and email with Leigh. It's up to me, what I do, not up to the T.V. I decided that this was just a little deal, not a big deal.

I tend to get really hung up on my routines. This reminded me of that day the mail didn't come and I fell apart. My routines are comforting, until they're disrupted. Then, they're binding. I don't want to be bound by my routines. I have to change my thinking from single paths to forks in the road. I have a very visual kind of brain, and I think of everything in pictures like that. When I think "11 P.M.," I think Alton Brown. When I think "3 P.M.," I think get the mail. Instead, I need to think maybe Alton, maybe something else. Maybe mail, or if there's no mail that day, maybe something else. I need to make my brain think in terms of forks in the road that go to different options, instead of thinking of a single point at those times.

I'm glad this is getting cleared up. However, I already checked, and my buddy Alton Brown is back on tonight at 11. Thank goodness.

For my first twenty one years, give or take, I felt restricted by who I was. I always felt like I didn't measure up to other people. As I learned more about myself, I learned to be comfortable with my strengths, weaknesses, and idiosyncrasies. I had something of a revelation one night as I realized what this meant.

Autistic Speaks blog post
18 May, 2010
My own skin

Being comfortable with myself means accepting in myself would I would readily accept in someone else.

It means learning what makes *me* happy, and as long as it doesn't hurt anyone, doing it.

It means learning to be careful that I don't develop compulsions… before I even start to develop them.

It means realizing that sometimes, I look different to people.

It means that sometimes, I *am* different from other people.

It means coming to grips with the fact that "normal is a setting on the washing machine."

It means doing what makes me comfortable, like cutting my hair off, regardless of what other people think of it.

It means watching what I like on TV, even if it's not age appropriate.

In fact, it means learning to throw age appropriate out

the window.

It means not getting angry at myself for repeating or throwing out bits of delayed repeating from TV shows, because I'm doing the best I can.

It means doing what I need to do to get through work, even if it means taking medication.

It means being an advocate for myself, at work for example. Everyone knows that I have autism and that I'm a little different, but they also know not to expect less work out of me for it. Oh, and they also know that I have a service cat and all about what she does.
It means accepting that God made me this way, not because of anything I did wrong, but so that my life may be to His glory.

It means sitting with the fact that people love me (yes, me) for who I am, and wouldn't want to change me even if they could.

I'm not there yet. Maybe it's normal stuff to deal with at 22, growing into yourself and whatnot. Give me another 10 years and we'll see. Maybe I'll be there by then.

My best friend Leigh was one year behind me in college, so for the year that she was a senior and I had graduated, I frequently went to visit her and slept on her floor. Although Leigh would object to this statement, she truly has the patience of a saint. Rather than get angry with me when I mess up, she looks for another view on the situation and uses it to help me.

Autistic Speaks blog post
20 September, 2009
Don't be a jerk. This is how.

This post would be written by Leigh if she weren't busy cleaning. I'm visiting her, and we just had a little mishap that she insists I need to blog about. She even gave me the title, so how could I turn her down?

Leigh lives in an apartment this year, and she and her three apartment-mates have really taken to decorating. As we were working on putting a pretty black ribbon around the top of the living room walls (to imitate crown molding, apparently), a cactus managed to basically frisk me. It caught the inside of the back of my shorts and pulled itself over, right up and out of the pot. It's a little cactus, kind of round, the size of a baseball, maybe. Still, it spilled dirt. After controlling my giggles, I crouched down to help Leigh reset the poor little guy and replace his dirt and…

I really knocked the whole thing over. This time, almost all of the dirt spilled out of the little pot, and more got on the carpet. I plopped down where I was and said, "Okay, that's it, not touching that cactus anymore!" Leigh sent me after the little vacuum cleaner, and I cleaned up the dirt around the floor while she once again reinstated our cactus friend.

Leigh says, "See? I could have gotten mad. It could have messed up our morning. But I just gave you another job to do that really did need to be done. I worked around it."

She thinks some people in my life need to learn this lesson about trying to work with me, and I agree. Rather than insisting I (or anyone!) do things I can't do, give me a job I can do just fine. Don't get angry, or "don't be a jerk," as Leigh says. Not everything has to be a big deal.

One of the most common questions I hear parents ask is, "How do I tell my child that he has autism?" After having answered the question nearly a dozen times, I decided to type out my response in a more permanent place (my blog). Children should not be made to be scared or fear or feel like something is wrong with them; instead, frame autism as a positive thing, something that makes the child unique, and he will think he's special (which he is!).

Autistic Speaks blog post
3 March, 2011
One idea for you

Does anyone watch *Parenthood*? I don't. I only watch Food Network. But, I did see a few clips of the last episode where Max overheard his father shout to his uncle that he has Asperger's. Later, sitting down with his parents, Max asks what Asperger's is, and his parents fumble around trying to explain. His mom cries. Max leaves with not much better of an idea about what he has, other than that he doesn't know anyone else who has it and probably feels very alone.

So now that we all know how *not* to tell your child about their autism, how do you do it? I'm just going to give you my take on it. You can take it, or leave it, or change it, or whatever you want to do with it, but this is what might have worked when I was younger.

"One of the best things in the world is that everyone is different. There are no two people alike (personally, I would say something more like 'God has created everyone differently,' but do with that what you will). We are all good at different things. Some people are really good with their hands, and they might become artists so that everyone can enjoy their beautiful art. Other people are really good writers, and they write books for everyone else to enjoy. Some people's brains make them really good doctors, and they help others by healing them. Everyone who meets you knows that you're really good at learning about different dinosaurs (random skill), so maybe one day you can be a teacher and teach people about dinosaurs. What are some other things you're good at? (let the child answer)

"Everybody has different things that they need help with, too. (random example) Do you remember when we painted the living room? I needed help from your dad to reach the high spots and put on the new wallpaper. That's okay that I needed help. Sometimes you need extra help knowing what to say to your friends (or staying calm, or sharing, or learning at school…. whatever applies), and that's okay too. We all need help with some things.

"But here's the really cool thing. Some people are a very special kind of different. These people are often really smart. They're really good at one special thing, like you and your dinosaurs. These people also might need some extra help to make friends, talk to other people, (insert things your child needs help with here). Doctors say that people like you, who have these certain strengths and weaknesses, have something called an autism spectrum disorder. There are a few different kinds of autism. The kind you have is called (insert specific diagnosis here, if you want). People can have a little autism or a lot and need a little help or a lot of help with different things.

"It's important that you know that autism is *not* a disease. In fact, it's not even a bad thing. It just means that your brain works differently than most people's brains. All of us in your family and your friends think that autism is pretty cool, because it helps to make you who you are. Some people with autism have done big, important things, and someday you can do those things too. That's what parents, teachers, and doctors are here for- to help you to be successful.

"Do you have any questions about what autism means or how it affects you?"

Personally, I could have handled this conversation by preschool age. I might have done better if my mom wrote it down and allowed me to read it, then gave me as much time as I needed to process and ask her questions. I remember when my mom had the other Talk with me (haha, I know). I was about 5, in preschool, and she didn't hold anything back. She gave me *twenty four hours* of time with her to continue to think and ask questions, and she answered every one. Do *not* rush your child. Allow him to think and process as long as he needs, then make sure he knows that he can continue to ask you questions for... well, forever.

Again with the "personally," I feel that a child should be informed of his autism by school age. If this conversation isn't age appropriate for a 5-year-old, either let me know and I'll see what I can do, or do what you need to do to make it fit your child, but please do not continue to hold off on letting him know because you don't know what to say or because he hasn't asked questions. If you wait for him to ask, it means he may have been ruminating on the issue for a long time and has finally decided to ask. You don't want him to wonder and worry about why he's different.

Of course, children are totally individuals, and you have to do what's right for your child. There's no way I can say that "age five is it," because each child is different. You know your child best.

People frequently ask me how I made it 21 years without a diagnosis. Aside from being female and having strong verbal ability and doing very well in school, part of the reason I slipped through the cracks is because I had ways of faking it. There is a huge, huge price to acting like someone you're not, twenty-four hours a day, seven days a week, every day of the year.

Autistic Speaks blog post
17 July 2011
No laughing matter

If you're not really, truly listening, please don't read this post. I mean it. Go away, please. It's extremely important, and it's not something to be read lightly. I hope you'll read it, and think about it, and come back here and tell me what your thoughts are. I'm terrified that I'll write this and scare everyone away and no one will leave me anything, but that's a risk I'm willing to take, because this is important.

It's been a typical Saturday. I'm on meltdown patrol, deescalating after a day that involved fasting bloodwork, out to eat in a noisy cafe, getting sick all morning from the small amount of gluten I ate, stopping at Mom's, going to get Mom's glasses, getting cat food, back to Mom's, and about two hours shy of church is when I lost my words and said that I needed to go home.

Mom and I were talking in the car on the way home (well, I was typing on my text-to-speech program, because Mom doesn't mind terribly if I type) and I said something to the effect of, "Loss of speech is not a result of anxiety but rather one of an overtaxed sensory system." Mom said that she understood that.

"So why don't they believe me?"

I could tell Mom tread carefully. Well, she said… you seemed so social and so happy in high school, you did so many things, silk line and performances and everything, and you didn't appear to have any issues…

I stopped her.

"I wanted to die."

You what?

For almost 10 years, I prayed every night that I wouldn't wake up to see another day. I didn't actually have the energy to kill myself, but if I had, I probably would have. I hated everything about my life, I was on the receiving end of so much cruelty amongst my "friends," I truly didn't believe that I deserved to live, and then didn't believe I deserved the relief of death at the same time. I knew this world wasn't made for me. I didn't know why, but even then, I knew it.

And *that* is what you need to know. You need to know that, at least for some people with autism (I've heard similar stories from other people), when you force them to be "normal," you make life not worth living.

So when I am pushed to speak even though I can't, when I am told not to chew or tic or flap, when I am told not to type, *that* is why I refuse to listen. That is why I fight back.

I deserve a life, too. It may not be what you think of as ideal, but it's mine, and I will make it my own. I am a square peg, and I will not be made to fit into round holes. It's time to start drilling square-shaped holes where I can fit. If you are here to help me in this, good. If you're not, I have no need for you.

I wince, I cringe when I hear of parents trying to quelch the autism out of their kids. Yeah, maybe we can learn to be "normal," to appear "normal." I could. But there was no *life* in me. I was devoid of… anything.

I won't live like that. I don't deserve to. No one does.

And so I won't. No more.

Be who you are, okay?

What follows is a series of questions. Some are questions that people ask me with great frequency, some are taken from parents who asked me to address a specific issues, and a few are questions that I have posed to myself in order to address an important topic. These explanations are meant to offer you a new perspective on issues parents face every day.

## *Why is autism considered a spectrum?*

The answer to this question may, at first, appear obvious in that autism is a spectrum of the severity of different disorders. Many people view this spectrum as a line from mild Asperger's disorder to severe autistic disorder, with PDD-NOS, which is the "catch-all" term for people who have symptoms of autism or Asperger's but not enough for a full diagnosis, falling in between. This is simply a fallacy. Asperger's, autistic disorder, and PDD-NOS are three conditions of varying severities in themselves. One is not "better" or "worse" than the other; they are different. I can practically hear someone shouting,

"How can you compare Asperger's/mild autism to severe autism? My severely autistic child's very life is threatened!" And the person who has a mildly autistic son or teenage daughter with Asperger's who is bullied and prodded until she becomes blatantly suicidal? What of that? Autism is, by definition, a severe and impairing condition, regardless of the specific label, simply due to the society in which we live. Rather than assuming the "other guy" has it better, perhaps we would do well to look for the similarities between and amongst ourselves, validate each other's struggles, and work together.

Autism is so much more than a spectrum of severity. Let's set that aside and consider that autism is also a spectrum of behaviors. Some people with autism flap their hands; some flick their fingers and some posture them. Most of us, typical people included, do something when we're nervous. Some people jump, some spin, and some slam their bodies into things. We all seek to regulate our confused senses. Some speak about the same subject with seemingly no end. Some, it's hard to get two words out of, and others don't speak at all. We all have issues with communication. Some people on the spectrum are friendly to everyone and would walk off with a stranger. Some have friends, but only online. Some don't seem to relate to people much at all. We all have social problems. Our behaviors are different, but they are all along a spectrum and that is what holds us together as people with autism.

Autism is also a spectrum of gifts, talents, and delights. I know of one little girl, who, while nonverbal, is always singing, a behavior common in those with autism. She comes from a strong, Christian family, and I think that singing is her way of praising God. There is a little boy who is hyperlexic and can decode dozens of words at just three years old. I know of another little girl who doesn't speak but writes the most beautiful poetry I've ever read. Some people with autism draw, some write, and some run. Some play, some tell jokes, and some build websites. Some accept people beyond any outward appearance but seem to see straight into their hearts.

I challenge you to reconsider the common idea that the autism spectrum refers to a diagnosis or a label. Look beyond that obvious to the nuances, beyond the label to the person behind it.

*What have you learned about yourself through having autism?*

Before I was diagnosed with autism, I knew that I was smart. Smart is good, but the problem was in that that's all I knew. If asked to describe myself, I would have said my name, my age, and my hometown. It's not that I lacked the vocabulary necessary to give a description, but rather I lacked the knowledge of my likes, dislikes, personality, and feelings.

Many adults with ASD report something of an "aha!" moment upon reading the diagnostic criteria for autism or Asperger's or upon hearing descriptions of them. I wish I could say that I had such a moment, but the truth is that I didn't even know myself well enough to recognize myself in the descriptions. Instead, it was a friend who pointed it out to me. It took a bit of explaining and giving examples of how the criteria fit me, because, for example, I didn't know that I was awkward or that I had some unusual language patterns or that I was no good at keeping up a conversation. I thought I was just like everyone else. I didn't fit in, but I didn't know that there was a legitimate reason why.

Over a few months, I considered some things. Why was it that when I got overwhelmed, my speech always shut off? Why did I seem to have super-human senses, from seeing spherical rainbows around all the lights when it was dark that no one else ever saw to smelling things that didn't bother anyone to my tendency to pick and chew on things? Why, from a very early age, did I hurt myself when I melted down? And, speaking of meltdowns, why was I still having them at age 20? I had to admit that ASD seemed the likely culprit.

I wish I could remember what my initial reaction was to being diagnosed with ASD, but honestly, I can't. For once in my life, I didn't become overly emotionally involved in the process and simply sat back and took it for what it was. In the months after being diagnosed, I was determined to beat autism and everything about it. I saw it as everything bad in me. If autism made me awkward when I spoke, well, I'd just have to be silent. If autism made me a bad friend (don't ask me where I got the idea that it did...), well, I wouldn't make any new friends. And if autism made me unable to read body language, well, I'd take out every book in the library on the subject. Oh yes, I would conquer autism.

It was about that time that I started my blog and became a part of the online autism community. I read from parents who wanted to eradicate autism altogether. I read from adults on the spectrum (those with autism expressed internally and those with it expressed move externally or visibly) who were part of the neurodiversity and autistic pride movements. I read about biomedical treatments, and behavioral treatments, and psychological treatments. At first, my reading was my attempt to find a way to work past my own issues. But slowly... slowly, I came to form my own opinions about what autism was and wasn't, and they weren't what I expected.

And somehow, in the midst of all this reading and learning and forming of opinions, I learned a lot about myself. I learned, for example, that I am extremely honest. I've been accused of lying for years, but I learned that I don't mean to lie; rather, I misperceive things and form erroneous memories, and then when I reiterate them, it sounds like I'm lying. But I am actually a very accurate reporter of what I've experienced.

I've learned that, though people have long thought me devoid of empathy, more or less, I can actually feel so deeply that I can't cope. I am sometimes so incredibly overcome by the pain, suffering, and hurting in this world that I simply shut down if I think on it too long. It's more than I can process. I also tend to process difficult situations on my own time. If I find out someone is very sick, for example, I won't feel a thing emotionally until I've come back home, sat down on my couch, had my bath, and put on my pajamas. Then, I'm liable to completely crash. So, I do feel, but not necessarily in the ways and timelines in which you expect me to feel things.

I've learned that there is more than one kind of smart. My previous belief that I was intelligent was not untrue, because I am very smart in terms of books and letters and dates and numbers. But there are some other forms of intelligence in which I am severely lacking. One example is kinesthetic intelligence, or being smart about moving. My gross motor skills leave something to be desired, to say the least. I trip frequently. I can hardly ride a bike. I can't wear flip-flops because I fall. Then, there is interpersonal intelligence, or being smart about people. With my communication deficits, I can't really say that I am interpersonally skilled. Now, it may seem disheartening to think of all the ways in which you're not smart, but somehow, to me, it was comforting and helped me to make sense of the world. I could now understand why people surpassed me when I had been "smarter" than them. They were smart in other ways, ways the world values quite a bit. The world made more sense.

I've learned that I'm very loyal, and that I'm emotional, and that I'm independent-minded. I'm quiet (except sometimes when I'm not!), opinionated, and stubborn. I'm immature in many ways, I'm a good writer, and I tend to get stuck on things. While autism is not who I am, it was the start of a path that led me to find out more about myself that I ever would have learned without it.

*Why are your memories of a given situation sometimes different than everyone else's memories?*

I frequently come away from conversations and tell my mom that I don't know why so-and-so is mad at me, or why they snapped at me or were rude. My mom says, "Lydia, he didn't snap at you." But I remember what he said and I know it upset me. In my mind, the man snapped!

Similar instances have been happening since I was very young, and for many years, my family thought I was lying. To be honest, even I thought I must be lying for a long time, because clearly I was getting things wrong. As it turns out, I actually don't understand a lot of nonverbal cues such as tone of voice, facial expressions, and body language. I can only see two facial expressions, actually-- happy and angry. Therefore, if someone isn't smiling at me, I think he's angry with me. But, he may have been sad, or confused, or sick... not angry at all. Similarly, if someone raises their voice, whether due to excitement or surprise, I always hear anger, and I assume it's at me. Over the years, I've found that it's much safer to assume someone is angry at you and have it turn out that he's not than it is to assume no one's angry at you when they are livid.

In addition to misinterpreting nonverbal cues, I actually miss quite a lot of language and especially when I am talking with more than one other person. With one person talking with me, I probably hear and process about 85-90% of what is said. With two other people, probably 70-75%. Three or more people, maybe 55-60%. I miss a lot!

Say I'm in a small group of three or four and everyone is excitedly talking about something that happened. They sound angry. Their motions are exaggerated, so they potentially look angry. I miss a lot of what's being said, but I do catch, "Can you believe her!" while looking in my direction, for whatever reason.

Later on, while talking to my mom, I might say, "Mom, so-and-so got mad at me and I don't understand what I said or did!" If we pretend my sister was there and can explain the situation, maybe she knows and can tell me that everyone was excitedly talking about something that happened at work the other day... yet I heard that they were mad at me.

*How do I know that my child loves me?*

      It has often been said that people with autism do not feel the full range of emotions that "typical" people feel. I would venture to say, however, that no emotion is entirely off-limits for a person with autism. In some instances, though I'm sure it's hard to discern which, I think that I actually feel more deeply and fully than many people do, such as with respect to animals. But, because I process and express emotions differently from others, people think that I'm not feeling anything at all.

      People with autism do feel love. Oh, we might not feel or express it in the ways you're used to, in hugs and kisses and words, but we do feel it. Your child might feel it in the familiarity of a bedtime story or in the comfort of the bath you give him. He might feel it in the deep pressure you give when you put on his weighted blanket. Some children might feel it when you engage in their favorite scripts with them. Your child knows you love him.

      But what of his love for you? Again, it may be atypical, but it's there, in its own unique way. It's there when he holds it together in school all day just to come home and meltdown; this means that he's most comfortable around you. It's there when he engages you in talking about Thomas the Tank Engine or dinosaurs, (or with my family, cats) because he wants you to share in the joy of his favorite subject. I express my love for my mom when I poke the tip of her index finger with the tip of mine; since hugs and kisses completely overwhelm me, I've devised my own way of expressing affection to my mom. It's there when I say "hi" to my mom for the third or fourth time in the hour she's been at my place. I'm just so happy to see her, but I can't get anything else to come out, so I pack a thousand thoughts and I love yous behind that "hi" and say it yet again.

It's there, if you know where to look.

On communication

*Writing is a struggle against silence.*

- Carlos Fuentes

*To be nobody but yourself, in a world which is doing its best, night and day, to make you everybody else, means to fight the hardest battle which any human being can fight; and never stop fighting*

- E. E. Cummings

# Autobiography

Arranger of sounds.

Syllables run freely.

The keys speak, confirming a notion expressed.

Once only a thought, now let free.


Author of songs.

Sung note by note.

Songs breaking through silence.

In monochrome.


Artist of freedom.

Effortless strokes of the keys.

Awareness so hoped for.

They're words that she weaves.

Communication has never been easy for me. So often, I've felt like I must speak a different language than my family and friends. It's so hard, so frustrating, trying to use my words to get people to understand what I want them to "get" from me. Like many people with ASD, I have a few stock phrases that I use with some frequency. You have to dig deep to figure out the meaning behind what I'm saying.

Autistic Speaks blog post
12 July, 2011
The many faces of kitty cat

If I had to put a number on it, like really had to, I'd guess that, on a good day, one out of every eight utterances is "kitty cat" or related words. On a bad day, more like one out of every three. But that's just a guess.

Why, you ask? What does it mean?

Sometimes it means, "I'm happy."

Or, "Thank you for making it possible for me to have

my cat, Mom."

Or, "I want you to say how pretty my cat is because I'm trying to make conversation but I don't know how."

Or, "I'm really getting anxious and I want to get home now."

Or, "I'm so excited I'm just bursting at the seams!"

Or, "I'm super nervous about something and I'm trying to comfort myself."

Or, "I'm sad and I'm trying to cheer myself up."

Oi vey. Er, kitty cat...

Imagine having many thousands of words at your disposal through your fingertips but inordinately fewer available through your mouth. Things like giving directions and explaining your thoughts and feelings become immensely difficult.  It becomes the listener's job to ask lots of questions so that she can understand what it is that I'm trying to say.


Autistic Speaks blog post

5 November, 2009

Life with a communication disorder


*I say*: Speaking is hard for me. Writing is easier.

*I write*: When I speak, it's kind of like walking around in a dark room with a flashlight. I have limited ability to see any obstacles in my way, but I get tripped up a lot and run into things that cause problems. When I write, though, it's as if someone has turned the overhead lights on, and I can clearly see the layout of the room and any potential issues.


*I say*: Boil it. On the stove. Not for 3 minutes, more than that.

*I write*: I don't know how to hard boil an egg, but I know how to soft boil one and I assume the process is similar. First, set the eggs in a pot of water. Turn the water on high and wait for it to boil. If you're soft boiling, when the water boils, set the timer for 3 minutes. When the 3 minutes is up, turn the heat off and douse the eggs in cold water until they're cool enough to touch. For hard boiled eggs, I assume you just boil them longer than 3 minutes; I just don't know how long.

*I say*: I like cats.
*I write:* I love cats because they're so calming and centering. The sound of their purrs and feel of their fur offer a sensory experience. They allow me to engage in a way that I can't with people, in a way that doesn't require words. Cats allow me to reregulate myself, every time I see one.

*I say*: Does it make sense?
*I write*: Do you better understand now what it's like to live with a communication disability? To have so much in your head and just not be able to get it out? To be so overwhelmed by the sensory world that you can't get past it to compose your words in speech? To have people treat you like you're unintelligent, because you don't speak like a very intelligent person? Will you keep this in mind then next time

you're talking to someone with autism?

Not only do things like giving directions become far more difficult with communication issues present, but I sometimes feel robbed of the ability to say what I want, when I want to… of the mundane, everyday things that people say.  From introducing myself to yelling at someone who cuts me off in the car, I often stay silent.

Autistic Speaks blog post
8 September, 2009
Words

Even when I can't speak, I still have so much to say.

There are the little words.

*I would like to walk to Dee's and see her dogs today.*
*Are you coming home early from work?*

*Hi, my name is Lydia and I am doing an autism walk;*
    *would your store like to sponsor me?*
*I don't want green beans tonight.*

Little words, but they're still important. Where is my
personality without those words, my wants, my likes,
my dislikes? I need those words.

Then there are the big, exploding words.

*I hate autism right now for taking so much from me.*
    *Hate it.*
*I'm extremely frustrated with my work situation. It's*
    *taking everything out of me, and I can't keep doing*
    *it. I was just in the hospital in June because my*
    *anxiety was so out of control; do you realize I feel*
    *nearly that bad again, just because of 8-hour work*
    *shifts?*
*Why isn't anyone really listening to me?*
*I'm desperately worried about my health insurance*
    *situation. Is this all because of autism? I repeat…*
    *right now, I hate autism.*

There are words that I don't quite know how to get out. I feel… is this frustrated, again? I'm not positive, but it might be. Why am I frustrated? Well then, I'm certainly confused. I feel the scary, explosive feeling that I haven't felt in months. I don't know where it's coming from. I don't know how to stop it. I don't even know how to get it out.

The words won't come out with my voice. I can get some out… *okay, I'm fine, ready?, stop it!* But that's not enough. You wonder why I don't tell you when things are wrong… well, where are the words? Give me the words, and I'll tell you! For nine days now, I haven't had the words I've so badly needed. When will they come back? I need them. I'm afraid my anxiety will get too bad if I don't find them again.

Aside from a couple of short Facebook conversations with Leigh, I haven't interacted with anyone since last weekend. I know that I have autism; according to one doctor I saw, I'm not supposed to care that there are other people in the world. I do care, and I want to talk to them. I want to talk to them so that I don't feel so trapped, so unable to communicate. I may not be able to verbalize, but I still have so much to say.

I spent my first eight or ten years in a constant state of frustration because I just couldn't express myself the way I could in my head.  My family noticed that, while I could discuss facts, I was unable to express feelings and opinions and I lacked social language.  When I learned to type in fourth grade, a whole new world opened up.

Autistic Speaks blog post
4 December, 2009
Words

I was made to be familiar with computers from an early age. I've been going on the internet since second grade, and I first started to use AOL Instant Messenger (AIM) in fourth grade. That was also the year I learned to type. By fifth grade I could type 80 wpm. I took to AIM like a duck takes to water. Looking back, it all makes sense.

Although I didn't have a speech delay, I've always had trouble with language. To be honest, I just don't sound like a very intelligent person when I speak. I'm not sure what it is. People have asked me (and I've noticed the surprise on their faces), "You mean, *you* went to *college*?" Yes, I did. I've only learned to express feelings within the past year or so. Before then, I just never talked about how I felt. My parents did notice that, but it wasn't exactly something they were going to take to the doctor, not knowing about autism. My mom says I've never been that great at conversations, either. Before I started taking Topamax for my migraines, I always tended to have one-sided conversations, she says. Now, on the Topamax, you're lucky to get a one- or two-word response out of me. I have a habit of repeating what other people say, too, when I'm excited about it. I wish I didn't do that, but I can't seem to help it. Sometimes, when I'm stressed, I get repetitive, and say the same thing over and over again. So, speech delay aside, I've always had some problems with language.

As soon as I started to use instant messaging, I noticed that I could say more when I was typing. It was like, instead of having x words at my disposal, I suddenly had 10x words. My parents were surprised at how well I wrote from an early age; I think what's surprising to people is the disparity between my speaking ability and writing ability. When I talk, it's like the words float around in my head and I have to peg them down to say them. I have to peg down each word to be able to say it. When I can't focus enough to peg down the words, I lose the ability to speak at all. That's what I call "losing my words." But when typing, typing the word pegs it down. I can refer back to it and go after the next word. When I've lost my words, sometimes I'm a little slower to type than I otherwise would be as I try to pick the words, but I can still do it. So far, I've always been able to type.

So, I love to use email and online chat programs. If I need to talk to a friend, I frequently text them "Facebook?" or "Skype?" and ask them to get on so that we can talk. I almost never (though it does happen, though rarely with friends, and I do talk to my mom and sister) choose to talk on the phone. I can't get my thoughts out that way.

If you have a child with autism, I highly recommend trying to teach him or her to type. You don't know what might be going on inside that mind!

Try as I might not to get frustrated with people who do irksome things when I'm trying to type, I sometimes lose patience in my head. I decided to type out a list of pieces of advice for everyone who talks to me while I type. After all, it's not fair to get annoyed with people without telling them how to do things the right way! It's important to note that everyone who types does things a little differently. Therefore, these directions might have some minor changes based on whom you're speaking to.

Autistic Speaks blog post
25 May, 2011
Some things to know about talking to someone who types

1. Only give me one idea at a time. It boggles me to have to respond to multiple ideas.

2. Please don't interrupt while I'm typing with new ideas. This confuses me; do you want me to respond to idea 1 or idea 2? I don't think you know, really, and of course neither do I.

3. Don't get weirded out if one of us refers to "talking." I *do* talk. Sometimes I talk with my voice, and other times I talk with my iPod. It's all talking.

4. Don't expect a normal pace of conversation. I type fast, but not as fast as you talk. Patience, grasshopper.

5. Don't be surprised if I sound somehow different when I'm typing. When I type, I am better able to express my feelings, wants, and needs... I will tell you if you've upset me or done something wrong; I will ask you to please stop this or that; I will tell you that something hurt my feelings. This is all normal to discuss, just maybe not what you're used to from me.

6. Don't tiptoe. If you bug me or upset me, chances are I'll tell you (or, more likely, hold my hand up)... point is, you'll know if I don't like it.

7. Normal rules of conversation apply. You talk, I talk, you talk, I talk.

8. Also, just talk normally! Most (not all) of the time, my receptive language skills aren't that bad (not average, but not horrible, either). If you're going too fast or if it's too noisy for me to understand... guess what?... I'll tell you!

9. Silence is OKAY! If you talk and then it's silent while I type, please don't keep talking... this will keep me from typing!

10. If you don't understand the device (because Heather—that's the voice's name on the device—can be tough to understand), just say, "Sorry, didn't catch that" or similar. I prefer not to just let you read because that takes away my voice, but in a pinch, that works.

11. Don't talk around, over, under, through… you get the idea… me. I'm here, I can talk. Don't direct questions to whomever I'm with, and please don't engage my mom or staff in extended conversation and just leave me out to dry. If you slow down and give me a sec, I can join in, too.

12. Please don't grab my iPod for any reason!

13. I do not like to be shown off. I am a perfectly normal 23-year-old girl, and I like to be treated like one and not a spectacle.

14. That whole finishing my sentences thing? So over that. Not okay.

15. Don't try to tell me that "it's just me!" or "you don't have to be anxious around me!" or anything similar. When I talk, I can talk. When I can't, I type. You don't need to be worried about why I'm doing what at whatever time. Most of the time, I have no idea why or when I'll have or lose words. Just go with it; that's what I do.

I was inspired by the movie *Wretches and Jabberers*. It gave me dreams of someday meeting my friends in real life (some of my closest friends, girls my age with ASD, I know only in the online world). When we sit and type on instant messaging, you would never know that we were anything other than typical girls having fun. It's freeing. Just like the autistics in *Wretches and Jabberers* sat together and typed, it would be a dream come true to sit and type face-to-face with my friends.


Autistic Speaks blog post

23 July, 2011

A wretch once more


*Sometimes you feel like a duck; sometimes you don't.*
- Me, attempting to make a point to staff the other day… almost, right?

This is one of those roll out of couch (because I sleep on the couch and not in my bed), don't even put my glasses on, wake up the computer and write, posts.

Yesterday, I watched *Wretches and Jabberers* with staff. For anyone who doesn't know, it's a documentary about two men with autism who do not speak much but type quite a bit. It's about advocacy, it's about making friends, and it's about changing lives. I loved every minute.

But it's left me thinking, if jabberers are people who speak and wretches are people who don't speak but type, what am I?

Sometimes you feel like a duck, sometimes you don't... right?

Today was such a good speech day. I didn't have words until about 3PM, but then they came and they stayed until 9 or so. That's six *hours* of words. That's huge.

And they weren't just "yes" and "nothankyou" and "Ihaveacat," either. Oh, no. There was some real conversation with my sister and my mom. Okay, so a lot of it was pulled from things I've written, but the fact that I could call it up and express it at all is awesome.

Today was a jabberer day, for sure.

But alas, to wretchdom I have returned. And at heart, a wretch I'll always be. Speech has never been and might never be my chosen means of communication. My speech feels metallic, airy, spindly coming out of my mouth… my typing is solid, true, and dense.

I don't type much about fear, which, if you think about it, is a funny thing, because I have so much of it. Speech makes me fearful. When you speak with words, you can't bring them back and rethink them… not least because I have little to no memory for speech after about eight or ten seconds. But when you type words, they are there for good, and you can always reread. You can't turn off your ears to speech, pause it, rewind it, and slow it down, but you can with typing. Not to mention that written words stay with me.

Well, now that I will only get 8 hours of sleep (the meds I'm on mean I need more like 12) as we are going to sensory-friendly Harry Potter in the morning, I shall try this sleep thing again and pray that no more posts write themselves in my head.

Duck or not a duck, a wretch I'll always be.

When I have a long period of time that I'm nonverbal or close to it, I collect thoughts and feelings and store them in my head until I can get to the computer. What follows is the result of a nonverbal day of collecting.

Autistic Speaks blog post
28 July, 2011
Ineffable

If I knew what to say, I'd tell you a million little things that I've acquired in my brain over the weeks and months and lifetime.

If I could, I'd tell you that I'm *so over* age appropriateness. You say Disney and American Girl isn't age appropriate for me? Well, excuse my language, but I say you can shove it. I would, if I could, ask you what the point of encouraging age appropriate interests is. Is it to make friends? I have many, even more than I can keep track of sometimes. Is it so that people will like me? Hate to break it to you, but people already do like me (not everyone, but, well, obviously, right?). Is it so that I can be normal? And to what end, I would ask? If I'm comfortable with it, you should be comfortable with it, and that's that.

And if I could, I would say that that I'm so over normalcy. Ask Chloe (my thousands-of-miles-away-autistic-best-friend whom I've actually never met!) what "normal" means... she'll tell you that it's "just a setting on the washing machine." I would argue that "normal" is of no value outside of its statistical meaning, which is the mean or standard deviation of 0. If "normal" means chasing down boys, going to bars, and trying to "get ahead"... all the while being unable to articulate your personal beliefs, values, and sense of self... well then, I rest my case, I would tell you.

If I could, I'd tell you that the peace that silence brings me is like a starry night and an open field. It's huge, it's wondrous, it's freeing. I'd tell you that speech is harsh, cold, and metallic. There is beauty in silence. Rather than run from it, try embracing it.

If I could, I'd tell you that I'm *still* stuck on some aspects of theory of mind. I simply cannot grasp that other humans have brains like mine that think thoughts like mine (this, coming from the girl who literally authors blog posts while she sleeps and dreams of typing). I can't grasp that people can think while other humans are present. I ask, again, how does the world not explode? I also get myself entirely confused when trying to figure out the essential aspects of a story which I must relay to another person in order for them to understand me. I say too much or I say too little, but rarely do I get it just right.

And if I could... oh, I'd tell you. I'd tell you that sometimes I feel like I ought to be doing a much better job of telling you what it's like on the inside, so to speak. I'd tell you that I have no direction, no idea where my writing is going, just that I need to write. I'd tell you that sometimes I think that a more interesting, more relatable, or even a more autistic person ought to be writing, and not me. I worry... I'd tell you.

I'd ask you how people are meant to sleep at night when the world is in such pain. Perhaps I don't show much empathy, but I literally lose sleep over hunger, pain, death... of people who have no faces and no names, of animals, of life itself.

And, I do apologize, but I would implore you... I would say, "Educate!" Tell just one person today something, anything about autism. Shatter a stereotype. There's a whole world out there, and it's ours for the taking, but we have to get past our shyness and educate. My place is at my keyboard,

57

and I thank God that I have found these keys and taught these fingers; where is your place?

I would tell, I would ask... I would even implore... but there are just no words, or none good enough. But then, words are all we have.

In the time since I wrote those posts, my life has gotten no less stressful. What has changed is the tools I have to cope with my stress. Now that I am much, much more able to process the upsets that happen on a daily basis—process, not ignore—I almost never get to the point that I lose speech. The "me" that writes once again melded with the body that for so long, refused to cooperate with my brain's direction to *move* and *do* and, for Pete's sake, *speak!* To give some context, I'm now in my first semester of grad school... studying writing!

Autistic Speaks blog post
17 July 2013
Creating joy

Life has a pulse to it, a rhythm.  I'm analyzing writing by autistic authors in terms of linguistic features so as to establish the validity of such a thing as an "autistic voice" in writing.  There are features, in our speech, such as intense metaphor and frequent neologisms that pop up in our writing too.  Whereas researchers frequently describe the traits as "barriers" to successful communication, I find that, in writing, they're little explosions of creativity.

Autistic writing creates an unusual prosody.  My autistic life has an unusual prosody all its own, I would argue, but these days, the prosody is monotone... but it's monotone in a way that is so beautiful so as to be endlessly pleasurable.

I write.  My days are filled with writing, from sunup (which, I'll give you, tends to be roughly around noon) until I peel my fingers from their home on the home row, force my eyelids closed until sleep takes me away.  I write extensive research papers, like the one on autistic voice, and another on contributions to British abolition; I write emails to network with professionals I met at the conference; I wrote book proposals, because sooner or later, I need to buckle down and try to publish something; I write essays; I write book chapters, and blog posts, and poetry, and music, and if I need a break, I chat on Facebook. For several hours each day, I put my feet to the pavement and go on a purposeful-yet-ad-lib walk, despite the heat, despite the rain. Even there, I cannot escape the drive to write, and my journal is in my backpack, just in case. There is always a case.

I marvel at the fact that one person can be so full of emotion and experience and connection. At 25, I live at the intersection of gifted and gutted–at the place where I might and do hear, "You… wrote that?" and "How do you not know this?" within the span of two hours. I've got the basic life skills down; heck, I even took out my own loans for grad school. People often comment that "you wouldn't know…" regarding the autism. For one thing, you may not know, which is why I'll tell you– because it's something I want people to know. Better you know now than in a moment of panic or social blunder, and better I tell you before you leave an encounter with your head spinning, wondering just what–who–how.– that girl can be that intense, day in and day out. All that aside, if you don't know, then I don't get to be who I am, which is a ball of quirks, sure, but also an advocate and a teacher. For all those reasons and more, it's best that you know.

But even if you didn't, if I didn't tell you, you would begin to make up your own explanations. I'm a bit of a verbal Tasmanian Devil, at times. I spin webs of words about all sorts of subjects, sometimes because the subject requires extensive explanation, and other times simply because it's fun. Often, my communication has multiple levels to it; I like to say things that are incredibly precise and yet not quite crystal clear, leaving room for interpretation based on your personal experiences. After a day with me, you would begin to wonder how one person can come up with the things that come out of my mouth, and yet be terrified of thunder and hot ovens and panic when she has to catch a ball. My gifts are real. So are my struggles.

After living for some time in a state of overload to the point that my verbal ability was overshadowed by my sensory processing confusion, I take great joy in the fact that, today, I can, more often than not, describe and explain my incredibly complex experiences of this world in a way that others can understand. I want to share them with parents, teachers, and professionals so that they can have positively, communicative interactions with the autistic people in their lives.

I believe the problem, these days, in my world, is far less about getting the autistic to speak than it is about getting her, for the love of all things good, to please. stop. talking.

In my travels online, people are always surprised to find out the degree to which I used to struggle with speech. I suppose it's a bit unusual to type so fluently but speak with such difficulty; though if I'm honest, it seems perfectly natural to me! Typing is visual and kinesthetic and remains intact despite sensory issues; speaking is auditory and is greatly affected by sensory dysregulation. The following are some of the most common questions I get about speech and language.

*Why can you talk sometimes but not other times?*

Many people have skills that aren't constant. Someone may be able to sing a high G one day but not another, or perhaps someone can run a 7-minute mile one day but not another. This is how speaking is for me; some days I can speak fluently, some days I can't speak at all, and most of the time I'm kind of in the middle of the two.

On a fluent day, people would be hard-pressed to notice that there is anything different about my speech. Maybe a speech therapist would notice that I don't really understand figurative language or that I am incapable of expressing my feelings verbally, but to the casual observer, I would seem quite typical (this is not to say that I am always conversational, which is another topic altogether!).

On an average day, I stutter a bit and get the wrong words sometimes and get stuck. A good example of this is last night when my mom called, and I said "hi" three or four times before I said asked her to "hold on please" and then asked her my scripted question. When she asked, "Anything else?" I said "hi" again. Now, I don't really want to keep saying hi. When I open my mouth, I have the question ready to go in my head, it's just that somewhere between my

63

head and my mouth, things get mixed up, and I get "hi."

And then there are bad days, on which I don't speak at all. As long as I have a backup way to communicate, like my iPod, I'm actually quite content to be quiet and don't really wish I could talk. Now, if someone were to come and take my iPod away, I would get frustrated very quickly and start to act out. The reason I can't speak is simple: I'm too overwhelmed by sensory input. For me, autism is, at its core, a sensory dysfunction. When my senses cross so that I see sounds and feel lights (synesthesia), and my skin crawls and my head throbs from the lights and the motion makes me dizzy, it should come as no surprise that my speech goes by the wayside.

There is essentially no predicting what kind of day I'll have, and even to say that they're "days" is misleading, as sometimes things change by the hour. If I lose speech, the best thing to do is to permit me to type, because if you don't pressure me, my speech will return at some point. If I feel pressured to talk, I'll worry more and more, and the speech will take longer and longer to come back. Patience is in order, and all will be well again.

*How can the listener help you to communicate verbally?*

    1. **Speak slowly.** I can only process one or two words at a time, so when people speak too fast, I'm processing several words behind what they're speaking, and in order to catch up, I have to skip over chunks of words. It becomes very confusing, very quickly. It's like reading a book with every fifth word cut out. You're trying to decode the first cut-out word as you continue to read, and three more have already gone by. Now you're just in a mess. If you speak slowly enough that I can process each word as it comes, then this mess will be avoided. To give you an idea, the TV goes just a bit faster than I can process. If you talk a tad slower than the TV normally goes then we'll be good.

    2. This may sound like I'm contradicting myself, but **please don't talk down to me.** It's definitely possible to speak at a rate which I can understand while not treating me like I'm unintelligent or a small child. I notice things like a very exaggerated tone of voice, for example, which many people use with

babies. This offends me, and I will grow rather frustrated quite quickly.

3. **Make sure you have my attention** before you start telling me something important. It's not uncommon for my mom to call and say, "Don't call me for the next half hour; I left my cell phone at home and I won't be there if you call it." I'll say okay and hang up. Ten minutes later, I panic because Mom doesn't pick up the phone. I never heard her, no idea what she said. The hard part is that I can even absentmindedly parrot back what is said to me and still not process it! So if you're telling me to do something, the best thing is to stay on the phone with me until I've actually done it. If you're giving me information, tell me to write it down, then ask if I've written it down.

4. **Don't speak for too long** without taking breaks for me to process and ask questions. If you continue longer, I will forget where you started and have no idea what we're talking about. (This holds true for when I talk as well... I frequently stop mid-sentence having no idea where I began.) If you're telling a story, tell it in short pieces and pause in between them, so that I have time to process.

5. If it's really important, or if you really need a complete and honest answer out of me, **ask me in writing or via email,** and let me answer that way.

6. Feel free to **ask me lots of questions** when I'm telling you something. I have a tendency to tell partial stories, leaving out things that really matter, and then it looks like I'm lying. For example, one time, I told my staff that I had a dental procedure done with no anesthesia. A few weeks later, I told her that I had the same procedure done with so much anesthesia that my whole head was numb. Clearly, she was confused. She said it took her a couple of weeks and a handful of probing questions before she uncovered that I'd actually had the same procedure done three times with varying amounts of anesthesia.

I know that the burden of sense-making (that's the professional term) is on the speaker, but when you're talking to someone with ASD, the listener has to take the brunt of the burden, or you just won't get anywhere.

7. If I happen to turn my back, walk away, or hold my ears, **that's your cue that I'm overwhelmed and need a break.** Just give me a few minutes, and I'll come back. I don't mean to be rude. I don't even

know that I'm doing it, actually. After a minute or two, I realize that I'm somewhere else, and then I gather myself and come back to the conversation. Please don't try to force me to continue talking if I've stepped away or otherwise removed myself. It will just end in yelling, crying, and pushing.

8. **Don't be afraid to ask me what I need!** Granted, I'll probably say "nothing" or "I don't know," but if prompted, I will type what I need from you. And, of course, this list cannot easily be generalized. Every person with autism wants and needs different things in a conversation partner, and the best thing to do is to ask the person directly.


*How can I help my child to communicate?*

Communication deficit is one of the hallmarks of ASD. Most people think of communication as speech, and if pressed a bit, maybe they'd consider nonverbal communication as well. But when working with autism, it's important, even vital, to consider all the other means of communication out there and to include in the child's day, every day.

Children with ASD range from being verbally precocious and like "little professors" to being completely nonverbal. As with all things, most of them are somewhere in the middle of the two extremes. I believe that all children with ASD should be enrolled in speech therapy, as even children who have good vocabulary often lack important social communication skills. So, first and foremost, work on speech, and often. If it appears that your child has no speech issues, consider whether he expresses his feelings or whether he has good social language that his peers would use. Dig deep.

But speech is not enough. I was one of those children for whom speech itself came easily, but language was another matter. I asked my mom, "How old was I when I first asked, 'How are you?'" "Still waiting," she replied. It's not that I don't care about other people but that I never had the language I needed to express interest in them. I needed to be taught explicitly, because I didn't pick it up from daily life like most children do.

My world was forever changed when I learned to type at age 8 or 9. I was never one to have a lot of friends in "real life," but from an early age I made and kept heaps of friends online, even ones from my own school. I had a tendency to develop friendships with people via chat, then when I saw them in school, I'd hide from them because I didn't know what to say. I was, essentially, typical when I typed. I could express emotion, and opinions, and yes, I could even ask, "How are you?"

In light of this discovery, my advice is that every child on the spectrum should have multiple means of communication, even if their speech is superficially typical. Older children might try typing. A parent might be quite surprised by what her child is able to tell her when he types. For younger children or for children whose motor coordination is such that typing is not currently an option, try sign language or PECS (Picture Exchange Communication System). There is a host of other means of communication that any person can use. Art, from the simplest scribbles, to drawing, to playing with clay, to making collages, offers a means of expressing oneself that speech does not have. Similarly, music and dancing reach almost all people on a very basic level. If a child cannot express his feelings verbally, he might be able to pick out words in songs that show how he feels or listen to classical music of a certain mood or even dance, expressing his feelings with his body. Some children who struggle with receptive language actually understand words better when they are sung.

Children also express themselves through play. Many children with autism seek order in their play by creating lines and other designs. I would argue that even this is expression, as the child may be seeking order in a world that is very confusing to him. It is important to teach the child other ways to play, but it would not be beneficial to deprive him of his natural way of playing, either.

There are as many routes to self-expression as there are thoughts and feelings and opinions to express. Look for opportunities to connect with your child in the ways he likes and responds to best. You might learn a lot about what goes on in his head.

*Are your speech issues lifelong or permanent?*

An old family video of Christmas 1990, just weeks after my third birthday, shows the aftermath of two excited little girls opening their gifts. In the video, I stand with my back to my nana, and she has me pulled in close. She's speaking into my ear, asking questions about the gifts I'd gotten and what I liked… and I stood there… and stood there…. There is an obvious blank expression on my face, as if the little girl standing amidst the Christmas chaos is present in body but utterly absent mentally.

This video is proof of some of my early memories, that I truly "went away," or, what I now know to call the shutdown I experienced following sensory overload.  Christmas was intense and it was a change in my routine—a good change, but still huge—and the result was that little brain simply could not take in any more input and so, it shut down.

In 2009, when I was diagnosed with ASD, I was a college senior.  Until that point, I had spent my lifetime forcing myself to just be *normal*, darn it.  Just *stop* being different.  It was like acting in a play, being someone I wasn't, all day, every day, for 21 years.  I finished my last semester, but when I came home after a lifetime of taking everything in, in, in and having everything I put out be like acting in a show… the shutdown that followed was proportionate to the length of time I'd been stuffing.  In other words, Christmas morning led to ten minutes of disappearing, but 21 years of faking it led to several years in which I totally regressed. One of the results of this regression was an intensified struggle with speech and language.

The best thing I could do to regain my ability, and the best thing any autistic person can do when life it's just entirely too much, is to let things rest. Just be. Continuing to force oneself to fake it will lead to total burnout, which is sort of what I experienced from 2009-2011. Now, in 2014, I appear much more capable and much "less autistic" (which is a ridiculous notion, as my autism is simply now expressed more internally than it is visible to others). My verbal ability, the way I speak, is much more like the way I type than it was during the hard years. I can still hear the autism in my own voice... the inflection that I didn't quite hit, the sounding like I'm reading out loud when I'm just thinking aloud, and the scripting about the kitties are all still a part of my life. This is a great example, if you can excuse the mention of entrails: A few months ago, I was returning from the doctor, having found out that I was going to have surgery to remove my colon. My mom and I were at the grocery store and she was just hanging up with my sister. I said, "Mom, did you say to her that they would take off my butt?" Sometimes, the words I have available at the moment don't quite sound typical, but, thankfully, my mom knew just what I meant!

I almost never lose my words these days because I know how to live so that it doesn't happen. I have lots of alone time. I do a lot of typing, which is my favorite method of communication. I get enough sleep. I socialize with people who allow me to be myself. When I have to communicate something big or important, I type and read my words aloud. I keep my sensory stuff in check. I catch issues at their start instead of letting them get so all-encompassing that I can't deal with them. I'm not typical, but I've regained a lot of my lost abilities from several years ago. I've found my balance in "living like an autistic person" and living like *me*.

'

Living like me!

December 2013

**On Life and Little Things**

*To live is the rarest thing in the world. Most people exist, that is all.*

- Oscar Wilde

Dichotomy

I am often

Only who I'm not,

But you don't care

So long as I have words for you.

You can't understand

(Through no fault of your own?)

That who I am

Is not the me you see.

Do you want to work on that?

They ask.

No, I don't;

I want to be free.

But in this world

The only freedom

Is to be

Everything you aren't.

# If I didn't have autism

If I didn't have autism, then I would be more.
I could go to work every
day.
I could make more money.
I could make my own way in this world.

If I didn't have autism, then I would do more.
I could sit outside on the Fourth of July and watch the
fireworks.
I could go out with friends after a long day.
I could go to the mall with my family, and still be able
to go out to eat.

If I didn't have autism, then I would live more.
I could travel to faraway places without fearing the
disruption of routine.
I could visit friends without worrying about how to act
normal for so long.
I could try exciting foods, go to concerts, and go to
movies without overwhelming my senses.

But if I didn't have autism, I would miss all the joy in life.
No hiding under sunglasses and a white hat.
No more weighted blanket after a busy day.
No more cats. No more cats?!

It's not an easy choice. I don't think it ever will be.

Today, I'll keep autism.

While autism may be serious business, and while looking on the bright side may not be my strong suit by nature, sometimes even I can find the humor in this life.  My mom and I frequently text, as I'm not much for the phone.  She could have called me and gotten three "hi's," an "I have a cat," and a simple "no" in response to her question… but she texted me instead, which gave me the ability to have some fun!

Autistic Speaks blog post

August 2, 2011

Just some funnies


*Look for my sunglasses please. Look good on floor*
*too if necessary.* (Text from Mom, 8/1, 1:32 PM)


Once I did some detective work and figured out what
"look good on floor" meant (in case you're wondering,
good equals "thoroughly" in this case), I did indeed
look.


*did you look for my sunglasses clip on?* (Text from
Mom, 8/1, 3:27 PM)


*I do not see them, sam i am. i do not see them in the*
*car. i do not see them near or far. i do not see them*
*on the floor. i do not see them in the door. i do not see*
*them, i'll be damned. i do not see them, sam i am.*
(Text to Mom, 8/1, 3:53 PM)


*Aren't you the clever one, now where did i leave*
*them?* (Text from Mom, 8/1, 3:57 PM)

I started my blog in the early summer of 2009. I wasn't sure where it would go or even what I was doing, for that matter, but I soon fell for blogging and, now, live life with a blogger's eyes. The following post is one of the first that took off.


Autistic Speaks blog post
12 September, 2009
Ten things, no questions


Ten Things That I Wish You Would Accept, No Questions Asked:


1. I can be surprisingly good at one thing (say, remembering conversations precisely as they happened many years after the fact) and surprisingly bad at another thing that you might think should be so much easier (like keeping track of receipts or remembering the procedure for filling a prescription).


2. Just because I have the words to type it does not

mean that I have the words to say it.

3. I really do hate to melt down, especially in public. If there were another way out, I would always take it.

4. I never play stupid. If I ask a question or say I don't get it, it means I don't get it. Please don't make me feel dumber by saying that I'm faking it, just because it seems straightforward.

5. What may be slightly bothersome to you, like the waistband on a pair of pants, can cause me to be a witch all day... or at least until I change clothes. If I'm crabby, it's because something is physically uncomfortable in the sensory realm of things. Until that thing changes, I will continue to be crabby.

6. I can't control my excitement over cats. So if you mention cats or point out a cat, realize that I'm going to get excited. Let me enjoy it. A little happiness never hurt anyone, eh?

7. I am often completely unaware of self-injurious behaviors. I scratch, hit, bite, and pick often, and

much more frequently when I'm agitated for some reason. In the moment, I don't know that I'm doing it; if made aware, it's so compulsive that I almost physically can't stop myself. But using my logical and intellectual mind, I know that I obviously I don't like the results of it.

8. I am exactly the same person inside regardless of how engaged (or disengaged) I am with the environment and others in it. Yes, you might have to change some things based on how I'm reacting in that moment, but please continue to treat me like the same person that I am.

9. Engagement and happiness do not depend on one another! I can be just as happy off in my own world as I am fully engaged with you. However, a lot depends on *you*, here. If I'm disengaged and you're forcing me to "act normal," then no, I don't feel very happy. If you're interacting with me in a way that I can in that moment, then I can be as happy as I've ever been.

10. While autism does mean that I am absorbed within myself (*aut* means self, after all), that doesn't

mean that I don't want you around. If you can come to me, rather than forcing me out of my world to come to you, then I'd love to let you in. There's a whole world in here... maybe you should check it out.

It wasn't until I began to compile posts for this book that I realized how very many of my pieces were written late at night. Looking back, I can think of a dozen or two times that I've gone to lay down only to have wiggling fingers and have to get back up and type something if I'm ever to fall asleep!

Autistic Speaks blog post
19 July, 2010
10 ways to help your child with autism

Well, 3 AM has come and gone. I just realized that I didn't take my PM meds (which includes melatonin)... and therefore I'm a solid hour away from any kind of decent sleep. I'm also ridiculously itchy (no, seriously, you have NO idea) because I was so attracted to the little colored sprinkle-covered cupcakes at work that I just had to have 2 of them, even though gluten and I don't get along. In the meantime, I thought I'd write some.

These are in no particular order (meaning, as they pop into my mind), though I will number them 10 to 1.

10. On a day when he is particularly hard to handle, make a list of the things you love about your child. Share it with someone (spouse, coworker, sibling, pastor, friend; if you're still stuck, heck, I'll listen). But how does this help the child? It reminds you of why you love him so much, reorients your attitude, reminds you of why you do so much for this little person. Your improved attitude will have a positive effect on your child. I promise, we can tell when you're upset with us.

9. Allow your child a chunk of time to engage in or talk about his very favorite thing with you, completely unbridled. People with autism spend so much time either self-redirecting or being redirected, that it often

feels like we never get to really dig into what we love without quickly being cut off or redirected. Personally, every time I talk about cats, it's overshadowed by the nagging thought that Leigh or Mom or Sister doesn't really want to hear about them. They certainly never *ask* about Elsie. So for a bit of time, just *let him be obsessed.* Obsess with him. Pretend that what you're hearing is the most fascinating thing you've heard all week. This subject is where he shines, whether it is bus schedules, the early years of the Beatles, or Thomas the Tank Engine.

8. Label emotions for your child early and often. Last night, an unimportant but abrupt change in plans left me frazzled. First things first; I picked up my kitty. Then I said, "Mom. I'm upset." No response. "Mom, did you hear me? I'm upset." The words felt unsettling. *"Mom*, I'm telling you something. I'M UPSET!" It struck both my mother and I that this was the first time… ever, maybe?…. that I'd come to her and labeled an emotion without prompting and without just acting out. This should not have taken 22 and 7/12 years to happen. Don't let this be the case for your child. Ask your child frequently, "How do you

feel?" You may need to offer suggestions or options at first, but never stop asking.

7. Model, model, model. Rinse and repeat. Model language, dealing with emotions, and facial expressions. Over exaggerate and explain, step-by-step, what you're doing and why you're doing. "Do you see that my eyebrows are pointing inward and how my mouth is puckered? My face is telling you that I'm angry." "Hey, let's get your new school shoes when we go to the mall to get so-and-so's birthday present. People say that we'll 'kill two birds with one stone.' That's a silly way of saying we'll get two things done with one action." "Oops; I expected the ice cream shop to be open. It's probably closed early because it's a weeknight. I feel very disappointed about that because I was expecting ice cream from this shop. But we can either go get ice cream somewhere else, or we can wait until tomorrow. Which would you prefer?"

6, Limit choices. If your child takes an hour to get dressed in the morning because nothing feels right, step 1 is to reassess his wardrobe and make sure that he owns only clothing that feels comfortable. Style comes second. That makes step 2 possible, which is to say "You can wear jeans or sweatpants today. Which would you like?" Do not allow him to pick any outfit from amongst 10. When you go to the store to spend his birthday money, rather than allowing him free reign of the toy section, say, "Would you like a game or some Legos? It's your choice." Obviously pick 2 things you know he likes, but do not allow him to choose Option C. Children, especially those of the autistic variety, become very easily overwhelmed with too many choices. For a young child, 2 is plenty. Expand the number of choices at your own discretion, but even as an adult, your child may struggle with this and need you to artificially limit his options.

5. Be flexible. If your child prefers to sleep on the floor rather than in his bed, simply move the mattress to the floor. If he complains that his pajamas hurt, let him sleep in his underwear. If he wants to watch pre-school directed television when he's 18 years old, who's he hurting? Realize that children with autism, by the nature of their developmental disability, show very scattered skills and abilities. He may be able to

drive like a 16-year-old, follow stories like a 6-year-old, read like a 10-year-old, and express emotions like a preschooler. Don't look at your child as the age he is but rather as the age at which he functions in each specific area. Cater to these as best you can, because your child *cannot help it.*

4. Use play to engage. If your daughter likes dolls, a dollhouse is the perfect toy with which to practice language, emotions, and interaction. If your son likes cars and trains, Thomas the Tank Engine characters have faces and speak and can be used to act. Many children like plastic animal figurines, which can be used in the same way. Encourage this type of play with an adult, older sibling, therapist, peers... all of the above.

3. Communication options. Regardless of how verbal your child may seem, teach him at least one alternative method of communication (PECS, sign language, typing, text-to-speech, etc). I was very verbal at a young age (2, 3), but the topics on which I can be verbal have always been limited. As I've grown older, I've learned to take fragments of things

I've either said in the past or have heard others say and piece them together so that it sounds like intelligible speech. It's really just complex delayed echolalia. Very little of what I say out loud is both my own and novel. In order to produce new ideas, I need to write. In order to process, I need to write. In fact, and this may not make sense, I often do not process what I say. I can piece the fragments together and form a response based on what I know I should say, but most often, it would be impossible for me to repeat what I've just said to you, because I never processed it. Part of my brain gets left out. Even if it appears that your child is keeping up verbally, if he is on the autism spectrum, there is a good chance that a second means of communication would serve him well.

2. Don't be scared of different. If I want to use a TTS in public and I'm not afraid of "what people will think," you had better not be either. If your child wants to wear clothing that he finds comfortable and you find unattractive, and you've explained that "people typically do not wear clothing like that. They may look at you and think you are strange" and your child has

no problem with that, then let him be. If he wants to text and wear headphones during church because it's the only way he can *possibly* stand to be in that crowded room right then, and you're afraid people will think he's rude, then I question why you're trying to impress *people* at church. If you know your child can only process auditory information when his hands are doing something (for me, it's Spider Solitaire on the computer), but it looks like he isn't listening, I ask you: Would you rather have him hear you, or look like he hears you?

1. Be consistent. If you're upset, stressed, scared, overwhelmed, or yes even exuberant, try your best to keep your expressions of intense emotion to a minimum. They may confuse your child. Children with autism need their parents to be the same. It's okay to practice labeling and expressing emotions, but only insofar as your child can understand them and can do the same for his own emotions. I am grateful for almost nothing more than the fact that my mom has always been rock steady in every way. You can use a lot of words to describe people on the autism spectrum, but "forward thinking" isn't usually one of

them… we live in the here and now, and if here and now is confusing or not right, then our worlds crumble. We can't see beyond the "right now" to the "what will be". We like routine because it's consistent, and we know what to expect; there are no scary unknowns. Bedtime needs to have the same routine, day in and day out, as does wake-up time, meal time, and time to go to the grocery store. It may be boring to you, but it will make for a much happier child. If something different is going to happen, please let us know what to expect and remind us several times. Check for understanding.

I don't have an intelligent way to end this, because an hour and a half later, my melatonin is kicking in… big time.

Takin' my kitty and goin' to bed.

Half serious, half just for fun, the following post summarizes the wisdom I've collected in my two decades of existence.

Autistic Speaks blog post

4 June, 2011

Lydia's rules to life

1. If your head becomes overly full with thoughts, tilt it to the side and lightly hit your top ear. The thoughts will fall out the bottom ear, thus clearing your mind.

2. The more complex the thought, the higher the likelihood that what will come out will be gibberish.

3. Most emotions lead to crying.

4. Before you buy it, ask Mom.

5. Poking and saying hi repeatedly both mean I love you.

6. A live bug outside is better than a dead bug inside. No bug is the best of all.

7. Consider others better than yourself. We (myself included) are often quick to assume that others are

wrong, when really, people often do what they do for good reason, so give them the benefit of the doubt.

8. If you got what you deserved, well, you'd be way worse off than what you've got, so don't say that you "deserve" better of anything.

9. Flappy *may* mean happy, but it may also convey any other strong emotion.

10. Cats make everything better.

11. Silence is golden. No, really; stop talking so much. My ears get tired of voices.

12. You can sit next to someone and not talk to them at all and just be. And be happy.

13. Speech is superfluous. Hearts are what matter.

14. You don't always have to ask me if every other thing you do is okay with me; I'll tell you if it's not in no certain terms (case in point: Leaving church tonight, Mom was clapping. In a lobby of people, I covered my

ears and shouted, "I HATE CLAPPING!").

15. If you want to end a conversation, simply say "I'm done talking now," or, "Bye" and then hang up or walk away. What's with all the beat around the bush stuff?

16. Try to act your age. When it really matters, try to act twice your age. And the REALLY important stuff, act half your age, if not less. You'll live longer. (Ask my friend Ann at church. She's 72, and she was running, jumping, skipping, and dancing through the sanctuary with ribbons tonight. She's very healthy and oh-so-happy).

17. Let your yes be yes and your no be no. See #15.

18. Be joyful always.

19. First person is confusing and its existence is a bit redundant. What's wrong with second and third person?

20. Leave things better than you found them. This includes Mom's house, the car, and the world in which

you live. Leave something better for your kids.

One of the very first questions I took from a parent is, "Where do you go when you go away?" There are as many reasons as there are instances of going away, but these are some of the recurring themes. As far as where I go... I go in.

Autistic Speaks blog post
2 September, 2009
10 reasons to go away

1. It's too loud
2. I've just talked to several new people in a row
3. There are more than a few people in the room
4. There's a lot of motion in the room
5. I've been socializing for a while
6. I have to pay attention to where I'm walking
7. Fluorescent lights
8. My clothes are bothering my skin

9. I'm trying to talk to someone in a room with other talking going on

10. Someone invades my space

Where do I go? I go away to where the world is only sensory, reduced to hard and soft, rough and smooth, hot and cold. There, scratching my hands until they bleed or hitting my head on a concrete wall a hundred times over brings immense relief.

Sometimes, I hide under the bed where darkness gives my tired eyes and ears a break. Other times, my weighted blanket allows my whole body to relax. Please don't try to engage me in conversation, because my words have been lost. All I care about is finding the right kind and amount of sensory stimulation to satisfy my over-taxed body and mind, in that moment. I can hear you, and if I try hard enough, I can understand, but it's no longer important to me. Just give me a break. Let me watch my fingers split the light in front of my eyes. Wait a while as I play with my Tangle toy (hey, I've seen you play with it too). Why don't you check your e-mail or make that phone call while I hide in the bathroom and hit my forehead with the back of my hand? It'll bring me back. I'll be back with you again. It might be a few minutes, or it might be a few hours, or it could even be longer than that. I'm sorry I can't tell. But just give me time, and I'll be talking again.

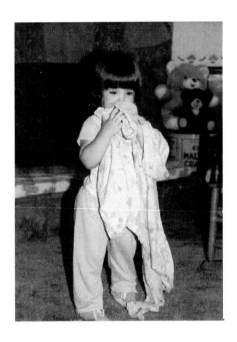

Self-calming

Lydia, age 18 months

As researchers try to search for the cause behind autism, sometimes more questions are raised than answers. I believe, as do many people in our autism world, that there are in fact autisms; in other words, there are many causes. In my own case, there are strong genetic components on both sides of my family. Autism is as different as one person is from the next, and my own autism is no different.


Autistic Speaks blog post
18 March, 2011
My autism

So, I read a lot online (and offline, in books). I read from so many parents, and it's interesting to see how parents look at their autistic children. There are two major camps that I see. The parent in camp A would say, "My son is NOT his autism. Somebody fix him. Somebody free him, please." They are angry at autism; they want it to go away. Parents in camp B would say, "My child is an incredible blessing of a person. People need to learn to accept him, because he has so very much to give." Some parents pull from both camps, and I'm sure some think something else entirely, but those are the two predominant viewpoints that I've experienced.

I want you to consider camp B for a moment. Have you ever noticed that, by the time children with autism turn into adults with autism, no one is saying how beautiful, hard-working, incredible, honest, pretense-less they are? The words I hear describing me are more like difficult, impossible, a behavioral challenge, frustrating, exhausting. My behavioral support staff (BSS) couldn't believe that I, a (her words!) "pretty, intelligent, friendly" girl, would have horribly low self-esteem. I didn't say anything, because my words failed me. But I can write it... are you kidding? How could I have anything *but* low self-esteem? Look at the words that are used to describe me on a daily basis. When that is what you hear day in and day out, what do you think I'm going to see in myself?

A problem that seems to keep cropping up with people who know me, even those who know me very well, is that they want to be friends with me until I... get autistic on them. Until I misinterpret them and think they're frustrated with me when they're not. Until I melt down in public. Until I can't work, can't go anywhere alone without panicking, until I communicate something very poorly. Then, they get angry with me, and their words can be harsh, and it's very upsetting. It ends friendships... many.

My therapist pointed out that I'm a bit of a paradox in that I simultaneously do not much care what others think of me while also caring so, so deeply that they like me. And when a good friend rejects me based on "the way I am," when it's just too much for her, it makes me want to stop being myself around anyone.

I wish people could accept some of the paradoxes in me. That I am at the same time highly intelligent and have no common sense. That I can write a book but can't interpret almost any nonverbal signals. That I can think on my feet but not speak on my feet.

This is my autism.

My autism is being too honest and hurting feelings.

Having so many words but limited ability to express myself, some times more than others.

Seeing the world, and people, in black and white.

Not understanding pretense and getting upset with people who use it overtly.

Having ridiculous anxiety, especially in social situations.

Needing, *needing* to hear about my cat, even when you're soooo tired of telling me about her.

Having immense changes in abilities from day to day.

And therefore never knowing what to tell you to expect (but, please, don't ever tell me I'm faking it.)

Being basically unable to successfully talk on the phone. Someone always ends up angry or frustrated or confused. Usually me.

Being furiously stuck on rules, whether my own or those imposed upon me.

Melting down, regardless of where I am.

Rocking, banging, hitting, flapping...

Misinterpreting everything... with a tendency to assume that no one likes me and therefore everyone must be angry with me.

Never "learning my lesson." In other words, I do not generalize well and need to be taught and retaught even if the situation is very similar to one I've already been taught.

This is my autism. Is it hard? Yes. I know it's hard. It's hard for me too!

But, at least to one person in this world, I like to think that maybe I'm worth it, not just despite, but in part because of it all…

As I explained previously, I try to make a point to be proactive about things that get on my nerves. One of these things is when someone says, "I have autism," and the listener's response is, "But you don't *look* autistic!" That's never the right way to respond. Here is one suggestion for when you're faced with someone who doesn't "look" disabled.

Autistic Speaks blog post
1 May, 2011
Please, spread the word

So, it's 11:40 PM around these parts. Do you remember the last day I was up this late? Okay, so actually, I do (January 4th-5th, 2011)… but that's beside the point. The point is that this is *late* for me. I've been out almost nonstop since noon. One panic attack and zero meltdowns later, I'm back at home, having swum, worshipped, shopped, shopped some more, visited with Heather and her cats, and who knows what else.

I have hardcore rituals that I go through, step by step, every time I sit down at the computer. The list of websites to check and updates to peruse is extensive (8? 9? sites), but tonight I will skip them *all*. Except one. Okay, two, because I did check email. I will come here and only here because what I have to tell you cannot be held back for one more day. It's *that* important. Your task is to spread the word on this one… Tweet, Facebook, blogs, verbal, I don't care. I don't care if you share the post or just the sentiments behind it. Tell your boss, your neighbors, your educators, your local politicians, your hairdresser. I don't care. Just tell.

So here goes.

At least for me, disclosing to someone that I have autism requires a very basic amount of trust. I won't tell just anyone. Yeah, sometimes I say it when I shouldn't, and sometimes I don't say it when I should. Come to think of it, I frequently get it backwards. But if

I say it, then on some level, you have some credit with me.

People respond in a variety of ways, but frequently, they say this or something like it: "You don't look like you have autism," or "I never would have guessed," or "You must be very high functioning, then."

Now, I'm not going to bash anyone for doing this, because first of all, they usually mean it as a compliment. Secondly, it's just a lack of education on how it feels to receive such words.

To be frank, I went through 21 years of sheer hell before I got a diagnosis and subsequent medication, therapy, services, etc. Horrible meltdowns, a ridiculously overwhelmed sensory system, lots of self-injurious behavior with the scars to prove it, suicidal thoughts and plans, tons of bullying, periods of random nonverbal times that no one understood… you get the point.

Then, even my "good" (read: not necessarily good in terms of happy but in terms of functioning level) days are hard won. I. Work. My. Butt. Off. to come across as "normal" as I can. I bite my tongue so hard it bleeds so that I don't have to wear headphones in church. I talk until I literally have to excuse myself to gag over the toilet so that I don't have to be nonverbal and stand out. I go into Target with Heather, because "normal" people do that and like it, and have a panic attack, sweating and shaking, but I put my hands in my pockets and put my hair up to hide it. All today, and today was a "good" day.

And yet today, someone (I won't say who it was, but believe me that if anyone should know better, it would be this person) told me that had they not seen my diagnosis in writing, they would never think that I have autism.

Can you say invalidating? What I've been and still go through because of this disorder… I don't know. I don't really have the words on this one.

Now, Debbie Downer as I might be at times, one thing I've learned and hold to is that I don't like to say "don't do this" without following it with a what you should do.

When someone tells you they have autism (or, heck, anything!) and you're surprised, do *not* say "Really?" or "You don't look/seem like you do" or "I wouldn't have believed that!"; rather, say….
(Do I have your attention?)

Say, "What do I need to know about how it affects you?"

No pity (and if I seem like I'm asking for it because of my lists of what I deal with, just, no. I'm not). No babying. No mollycoddling.

Education.

So, now you know, and now I turn you loose to tell anyone who will listen.

One of the things I really have trouble with is being present in a moment. I have a tendency to go away. Sometimes I even have conversations when I'm not really there, and then I have no memory of them. The issue is that I become so sensory – overloaded that I lose continuity. I experience the world in windows- flashes of times and places and moments of revelation. It's fitting, then, that I'm a blogger, as windows to my world are the way that I connect to it.

Autistic Speaks blog post

August 3, 2011

Windows

For perhaps the eighth or tenth time in the year it's been since I moved here, I shall sleep in my bed. I am desperately in love with my couch, but it's kind of broken (Mom says it's "sacked out," whatever that means), and some nerve in my back was shouting at me. So, to the bed I go, now. This will be night... two? Three? The last two nights went well, but tonight it's going on 1 AM and I still have blog posts rolling around in my fingers. Oi vey.

Do you mind a bit of musing? I thought not. Buckle up, then.

As I said not terribly long ago, I worry. I worry that I am too small a person for too big a job. I worry that I will never be good enough or eloquent enough or find the right words to tell you what autism is really like. I worry that I will step on toes, because most of the bloggers I interact with are mama-bloggers, and while I don't for one second even fathom that I might know what's better for their child than they do, I worry that at some point I'll come across like I think that I do. I worry about fitting in. And I worry about continuity; when I read other blogs, there are links and themes that run from one post to the next to yet another… and I worry that all I have for you are windows.

Are windows enough? They're all I have. So, tonight, as we close in on 1 AM and I sit here without my glasses on, I will offer you one more window (the 370th one since I began writing this blog over two years ago).

One of the things we work on around these parts is emotion identification. This often takes the form of watching the ever-popular sitcom *Friends*, which frankly, has always gone a bit over my head. But, with someone there to watch with me and explain the funny parts (which, on more than one occasion, has bordered on rather awkward, by nature of the show), well, I do all right, and if I'm in the right mood (which is often), it's fun.

But I was thinking (and, I tell you, my fingers were literally trying to type while I was laying in my bed… you think aloud, I think atype, right?) that perhaps my issue is not one of lack of empathy, feeling, or knowledge, but rather… a difference of language.

What do you call the corner of exasperated and defeated?

It sits at the crossroads of frustrated and confused.

It's when you need big, open spaces but you have tight corners.

And it's when you want starry skies but you have a thick, dense, low fog.

It's squinting through murky waters to see what's just beyond.

It's feeling like your fingers are tied down (or for you, like your mouth is taped shut).

I could go on, but my point is this: I know exactly what I'm feeling, and I can (if I'm typing) perfectly describe it to you. No, I can't sum it up in one nice little word like you might, but I can certainly explain how I feel, can't I? And, correct me if I'm wrong, but can't you get some semblance of sense out of what I just described?

It's unlikely that you'll ever hear me use feelings words verbally, and it's none to forget about it you'll hear me really describe it like I just did out loud. My brain just doesn't work that way... it works with my fingers instead of my mouth.

111

But if you're willing to let me type, go ahead and ask me what I'm feeling. Give me a moment to ponder. I have no problem letting you know.

I just can't promise it'll be what you're used to, eh? (Have I mentioned that my typing is picking up Canadian bits and pieces? It's like copying someone's style of speech, only autisticly.)

All right, folks. The blinds are down, the curtains drawn. And, back to that musing, I suppose the way I experience life is as a serious of windows. My memory isn't the best anymore, and my sensory system is uh, whacked, and that leaves me with very little continuity in things. I function in boxes and windows.

Perhaps a blog and the windows it offers you are an appropriate medium by which to share myself and my life.

Now, would someone tell my fingers to go to bed already? Take two, we shall.

A dear (online!) friend, and autism-mama, has told me that the everyday is the most interesting to read about when it comes to autism. I get a lot of questions about how I do things, from remembering prescriptions to cleaning my apartment. The following are some questions people have asked about the mundane things in life with ASD.

## What do you like about having autism?

For so many years, all I wanted was to be a normal girl. I yearned to be just like everyone else. I never stopped to consider what "normal" meant. "Normal" is not just going to parties, having fun, and laughing a lot. No, normal maybe also be gossiping, doing whatever it takes to get ahead, "experimenting" in all its glory, and being unable to articulate who you are and what you stand for.

Why would I want to be "normal," then, when I can be who I am? There is no room for gossip in my world, because none of my friends even know each other to gossip about. I don't work, so there is no getting ahead in business. I've never felt the need to experiment with, well, anything people normally experiment with. And, after a lot of searching and many years of having no idea who I was, I now know exactly who I am and what I'm about.

People have some funny ideas about autism. One of them is that autism is all bad and that nothing good can come from it. If one of these people looked at my life, he might point out the self-injurious meltdowns, the periodic inability to communicate verbally, and the extremely limited diet I need to stay healthy. But if autism is what makes me able to write like I do, if it brings me the joy of the rainbows around the nighttime lights, if it makes me so determined to be everything I can be, well then, I think the benefits outweigh the drawbacks.

I like...

- the way I can absorb and experience the music at church and not have to sing a word.
- the way, when I go to bed with a blog post on my mind, I wake up in the middle of the night with my fingers literally trying to type it out
- the way just the thought of a duck leads to cracking up.
- that cats can fix anything.

- that playing in water brings complete inner peace.
- not being what people expect
- knowing exactly who I am... and realizing that I can't know exactly who other people are (in other words, I like that I don't make snap judgments, as much as I can avoid them).
- that, at 23, I maintain many of my childlike qualities... trusting, seeing the good in people, and innocence.
- that while I can almost never remember what I did yesterday, I can recite blocks of text and poems I learned ten years ago.
- that I have an insider's view of what many people consider to be a mystery, and for that, I consider myself quite blessed.

*Can you explain what your sensory issues are like?*

Once in a great while, I'll sit back and think, "Wow. This must be what a typical body feels like all the time." It happens about once every few months, if I'm lucky, and it only lasts a few seconds, then it's back to the daily grind.

But what is the daily grind of an autistic body? To start with, on a good day, I itch from head to toe. Even my eyeballs itch. On a bad day, I feel like someone is taking a cheese grater to my skin. So if you wonder why I scratch and hit myself (although I've learned not to do it when people are around because it upsets them, so imagine how uncomfortable I am), it's to stop the itching and burning. It appears to be unrelated to clothing, temperature, chemicals.

Sometimes my body feels too tight. That's when I need to have a bath or swim, and then I feel better. Other times, it feels like my molecules are floating away from me, and I need deep pressure from my weighted blanket. If said blanket is not available, I will hit or punch myself repeatedly, until my molecules tighten back up. Now, I know my molecules are always just fine, but that's the only way I can think of to describe it.

Again, on a good day, fluorescent lights give me migraines after an hour or two and loud sounds hurt my ears and upset me. So, what of a bad day? Well, the older I get, the more my senses get mixed up. On a bad day, the lights burn my skin (feels just like a sunburn blistering) and ring in my ears like metal. The sounds sit in my throat and my chest. The motion (whether it's cars or people walking in the store or simply the colors of all the stock on the shelves) makes my head feel like it's being electrocuted, and I can't find my feet on the floor.

When posting on a forum one time, I said that I could drive a car but not cross the street on foot, and someone told me that that was impossible. It is certainly not impossible, and I will explain why. When I am in my car, it's like being in my apartment; my senses stay straight and my molecules are in order. I can see the cars moving, and while it's not easy and I hate doing it, I can drive across the street. When I'm walking, I've got the sound and motion of the cars passing, the smell of the exhaust, the feel of the breeze on my skin... and there you've got the head fog going on. The outdoors and some stores bring on a certain kind of sensory overload that causes my head to fog up. I can't think straight. This is why I tend to walk out in front of cars or cross streets without ever looking up, because I am foggy. The head fog is also responsible for leaving the stove on when I'm done cooking, or answering questions on the phone without having any idea what I've said. That head fog, it can be dangerous.

I wish I could take an "autism cam" into a store with me and so I could show everyone what a store is like. I'll use the other night as an example, when my mom took me to a department store. First of all, the clothes and other items were so visually loud that my hearing was drowned out. It sounded like I was underwater. Because I don't have a very good sense of where my body is in space, in my mind, the racks of clothes kept jumping out and getting me, and it hurt. The floor looked crooked and was hard to walk on. Add to that losing my mom and then, once I found her, she was practically on top of me, and I admit that the result was some yelling and some tears. I probably looked like a little kid throwing a tantrum, but imagine going into a fun house with black lighting and the music blaring, and then losing the people you're with. You might melt down too!

Lest you think that every sensation leads straight to meltdown, there are quite a number of sensations that I crave. I love sensations that put my molecules to rights, such as deep pressure or spinning or fast movement. I love rides at the park, including roller coasters. I love the cool place on my pillow at night. One of my favorite places to be is on my couch, which, while kind of broken, brings me immense comfort. I like to wedge my head into the corner of it, putting tons of pressure on it. My absolute favorite sensation is my cat in my face. It may sound odd, but I like to pet her with my face. Oh, there's nothing better.

Imagine living in 1939, in the era of black and white films. With the first showing of *The Wizard of Oz*, the world changed. Suddenly, everyone knew what color film was, and black and white films seemed not highly entertaining but kind of boring. Life with autism is similar. Because I know what it's like to have hypersensitive senses, I know what the explosion of stimulation that is Technicolor feels like. The rest of the world lives in the equivalent of pre-1939, only having experienced black and white. Essentially, typical people don't know what they're missing in terms of the sensory world. But for me, since I've experienced the world in its super-sensitive-autistic-glory, black and white leaves me yearning for something more.

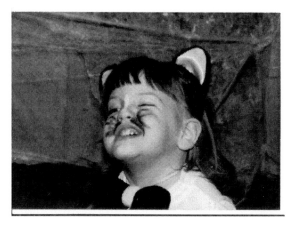

Face paint (including makeup!) assaults my senses
Lydia, age 2

### Why could you do x yesterday but not today?

A situation might go something like this: You see me out driving. Then, a week later, you see me and ask me if I'm going to go to, say, an event downtown. I say, "No, I can't drive." You would be confused, because you just saw me driving, right? You might think I was lying, even.

The fact is, I can drive some times but not others. And yes, on occasion, I go somewhere then have to wait a long time until I can go back home because I can't drive. The issue is basically sensory.

If my senses are in order, then I can drive, although I don't do highways, bridges, or tunnels, and I can never go somewhere Mom hasn't shown me a bunch of times already. But, if I'm having a wacky sensory day, which is a lot of the time anymore, then driving is out of the question. So, when I say, "No, I can't drive," in reference to the event downtown, I might have meant that my senses are currently such that driving is entirely impossible, or I might have meant that it's Mom's car and she doesn't permit me to drive downtown, or I might have meant that, even if I wanted to, going downtown involves highways and bridges, so I can't handle going there.

Issues come up all the time where people don't understand why my abilities fluctuate rapidly. Why did you speak to me yesterday but today you're typing? Why could you run into the store to pick something up yesterday but today you need someone to go in with you? Why could you carry on a conversation with me yesterday but today you're far from conversational? Why did you answer my questions yesterday but today you're repeating them? Why did you seem like you had Asperger's yesterday and today you seem quite autistic? Why, why, why?

121

Because, basically, I'm a human, and I'm an autistic human. Maybe yesterday my senses were straight, or maybe you saw me in the morning before the day has taken its toll, or maybe the stars were aligned just so and I could do whatever it was. Never, ever, get upset with a person with ASD or accuse them of faking anything just because their skills fluctuate from day to day. Instead, take each day as it comes, and follow the person's lead on what they need from you to be most helpful to them.

*What goes through your head before and during a meltdown?*

As much time as I've spent analyzing and considering my meltdowns, I have made little to no progress in heading them off at the get-go. This is frustrating. The issue, I think, might be in part that there are as many types of meltdowns as there are reasons for melting. So, if I have a meltdown because the Food Network froze up, I might be able to slow down the melt the next time it freezes. But if, say, the Food Network changes its schedule? That's another matter altogether and is cause for another meltdown.

There are a few different kinds of meltdowns, though. The first, and the worst kind, are the ones that build all day. They're... sensory dysregulated, usually in addition to having forgotten meds that morning, followed by a thunderstorm, followed by getting too hungry, and then when Food Network freezes? Bam. Meltdown. It's likely to be a marathon meltdown, too, one that lasts for hours and hours. My head isn't thinking anything for a while – it's totally short-circuited. Then, after a while, I ruminate on each thing that went wrong and upset myself over again, over and over. The best way to head off one of these is to take time to process each little thing as it happens rather than putting it off to process later. Essentially, I need to allow myself to have five or six smaller meltdowns rather than one really bad one.

Another kind of meltdown happens over interpersonal conflict, either real or imagined. Whether I think someone has snapped at me, or a friend is unhappy with me for some reason, or someone in authority has found me disrespectful, these are all reasons to melt. During these times, what goes through my head is how I'm a horrible friend/student/employee. I get angry at myself, and this causes me to melt down. Again, I tend to ruminate over what was said or what transpired, and I usually talk to my mom to get sorted again.

Finally, I frequently melt down due to something going differently than I expected it. This can be a change in plans, something being cancelled, or something being sprung on me at the last minute. These are usually shorter meltdowns, because once I change around the visual pictures in my mind, then the new way becomes "right" and I'm back in business.

Meltdowns are not easy things to explain, because by their very nature, I'm not thinking clearly when they happen. It takes a lot of time and trial and error to figure out how one's meltdowns start, develop, and what can be done to help them end sooner.


*What goes through your head when you're in water (or otherwise stimming)?*

There are as many ways to stim as there are people with autism. I think that, regardless of how we go about our stimming, the act itself strikes a similar chord in all of us. Some kids spin, some flap, some flick, some squint, some poke, some pick... for me, right now, it's water.

Everyone has a nervous habit, right? People bite their nails and shake their legs and whatnot. These are grounding behaviors. I'm sure that "grounding" has a technical definition, but I think of it as the behaviors that serve to tie me down to earth when my body wants to float away. We autistics frequently feel like we're floating away, whether it's because we don't understand our surroundings, or we can't express ourselves, or our senses are out of whack and we can't fix it. Just like typical people engage in grounding behaviors when they are nervous, upset, or uncertain, we do, too. It's just that our behaviors look a little different and are labeled "stimming."

When my senses are a mess, or when my molecules are floating away, or when I'm confused, I need to ground myself, and I use water when I can. I love to swim and take a therapeutic swimming class a few times a week, but in the absence of swim time, I just get a bath. If there's no time for that, I turn the faucet on.

And my mind goes blank, save for a tiny bit of

125

underlying current running through it, which lets me know that I'm still alive. There are no words, no sounds, no pictures – nothing. Just that little buzz, and without that buzz, I would question whether I were even still here. At the same time, I feel more alive than ever. I feel in touch with my environment in a way I usually lack.

Maybe this explains why I don't like to be bothered when I'm in water. No talking, no listening, no looking. I just like to be.

Stimming by picking at my fingers, as I still do today

Lydia, age 2 and sister Emily

**On Faith**

*Be faithful in small things because it is in them that your strength lies.*

- Mother Teresa

*Faith in the sense in which I am here using the word, is the art of holding on to things your reason has once accepted, in spite of your changing moods. For moods will change, whatever view your reason takes.*

-C.S. Lewis

Spring (written at age 8)

Have you ever heard a bluebird twitter,

As it's kissed by the morning sun,

When skies are blue and grass is green,

And spring has just begun?

The rolling hills rise before me,

Streams tumbling to the ground,

And the cool, soft breeze blowing

Is the only sound.

Lying on the ground,

I find myself thinking this:

Does mother nature know

How wonderful she is?

# Conversation with a Tree

The unchanging days pass namelessly

From my perch, adorned in rosy garb

Unsuspecting, I note a lofting tree,

Rooted in the yard.


I don't know whether it is oak or pine,

Nor whether it stands small or great,

If it's offered shade for a century,

Or held climbing children by its weight.


The striking chord of my friend tree,

Is not the former nor the latter,

But the fact that she stands outside the window;

For her roots are all that matter.

Some have roots to another person,

Some have them within four walls,

Some might move them periodically,

I thought I had no roots at all.


For I haven't any person,

I haven't any home,
I haven't any... Anything,

To call my very own.


I looked at my tree and chided her,

How dare you mock me so?

You tantalize me with your roots,

Right outside my window.

My tree, she answered, timidly,

Oh, friend, I never meant you harm,

I only meant to give you cause,

To pause and make your heart grow warm,


For when I look at you, I wonder,

What it must be like,

To have roots in a Person,

One made of Love and Light!


One Who will never leave you,

Nor of your musings tire ever,
One Who is always with you,

In Whom you might find rest, wherever.


I found myself quite lost for words,

Apologetically, I said,

My tree-- I had no idea,

And this is what she plead:


I bid you, when you look at me,

That you promise to recall,

Your sweet Savior, ever there,

The deepest Root of all.

My faith and my autism are forever and completely entwined. For so many years I believed that I was somehow "less than," but last year, I had a realization that, while I was in no way "more than," I was decidedly different, and in a good way.

Autistic Speaks blog post

1 August, 2010

Not despite. Because.

*You are to be holy to me because I, the LORD, am holy, and I have set you apart from the nations to be my own. (Leviticus 20:26)*

Tonight at church, the pastor was preaching on Hab…Haba…(help me, Google)… Habakkuk (thanks, buddy). We're doing a series on it, and tonight he began to describe the judgment that God was going to pass on Israel via the even *more* evil Babylonians. I was doing my best to follow along, when something he said caught my attention.

"Israel, you were supposed to be different, holy, set apart."

And that made me think. Usually, when I think of myself and my differences, my "otherness," I think of it as a bad thing or something that needs to be changed. Rocking in church? Better stop it. Stimming at the lights at the Broadway showing of *Hairspray*? Quit that. Greeting new people with "Hi, do you like cats?" Not exactly socially appropriate.

133

But autism isn't the only way that I'm different. If "normal" for my age is going to bars, smoking, and having sex, (that's the stuff the girls my age at work go on about), then I'm glad I'm not normal. I don't drink, or swear, or date, or wear revealing clothing because God has called me to be set apart from my peer group. I'm not saying that it's wrong for everyone to drink and date and whatnot, because I don't know what God says to other people – I can only speak for myself, and what He has called me to do and be.

Rather than thinking of my autism in the negative, maybe it's time to consider the ways it contributes to my holiness, which, after all, is what I strive to be (not saying I succeed, though). Because I'm kind of stuck in childhood, I'm not tempted to watch sex, swearing or violence on TV or read it in books or see R-rated movies. I'm not tempted to be sexually inappropriate. And getting drunk and doing drugs is so far off my radar, I've never even been in a bar or seen a drug, let alone wanted to try them.

While most people in their 20s have outgrown their childhood innocence, I'm pretty sure most of mine remains intact. I'm certainly more sensitive to the injustice and inhumanity of the world than a lot of people I know (for example, I often cry when I see animals dead on the road, even if it's a skunk).

And if God is calling Christians to be set apart, other... holy... then maybe rocking, stimming, and questions of genuine interest (rather than the obligatory "how are you"s) aren't so bad either, eh?

Maybe God *created* me to be this way. (Different. Other. *Autistic.*) Maybe He did it as a way of mirroring His own holiness in one of His creations. Or maybe He knew that, without the autism, I wouldn't be able to stand up to the temptation that surrounds me.

What I'm saying is what Leigh has said so many times, but now I'm coming to understand for myself, now that I have some explanation behind it. I've always thought of autism as being something that is all bad, but that God can use for good. But now I'm starting to see that maybe He actually *made* it for good to begin with. Good not despite of autism, but because of it.

I want to succeed in my work not despite of my autism but because of it.

I want my family and friends not love me not despite of my autism but because of it.

I want to be set apart not despite of my autism but because of it.

And most importantly to me, I want to be Godly not despite of my autism, but because of it.

I think I'm starting to understand…

Whether you think of it as a spectrum of humanity, a piece of the puzzle, or a part of Christ's body, we each have our own unique sets of gifts and talents. The following post was written as I truly came to understand that every color of the rainbow, every piece in the picture, every toenail and eyelash are necessary to make the world complete.

Autistic Speaks blog post
13 September, 2010
On your mark

So since we find ourselves fashioned into all these excellently formed and marvelously functioning parts of Christ's body, *let's just go ahead and be what we were made to be*, without enviously or pridefully comparing ourselves with each other, or trying to be something we aren't. (Romans 12:8ish, The Message)

Okay, so I realize that I don't write exclusively to a Christian audience, but I think everyone can glean something important from the above verses, don't you? Especially the italicized part (that's why they make italics… to emphasize or drawn attention to a certain word or phrase, eh?).

Now that I'm done cracking myself up (and I'm doubting anyone else thought it was funny)… I can hear your head, saying, "Lydia, make your point already!"

I'm Lydia. I'm not Mom, I'm not Sister, I'm not Leigh, and sadly, I'm not Elsie. That means that I can only be what *I* was created to be and glorify God the way that *He* intended for *me* to do so. I can't try to grow flowers like Mom and wonder when I come up failing. I can't try to live my life like Sister, with her NYC clothes and money, and wonder why I fall short. I can't try to relate to people like Leigh and then wonder why it doesn't work.

Perhaps closer to home, this also means that I can't try to have boyfriends like seemingly 98% of my peers, can't try to work full time like most people and earn lots of money, and can't try to take jobs any number of miles from home, like a lot of people I know have done in the year or two after college graduation. I can't try to get married, have babies, get a dog, teach... the list goes on.

But here's the thing (isn't there always a thing? I seem to say that a lot...).

I can help mothers, fathers, sisters, brothers, and teachers reach seemingly unreachable children. None of my friends do that.

I can comfort a cat whose only comfort is the fact that, wherever it goes, it still has a litter box (and will even sleep in it for security). I can love each and *every* cat at work as an individual, in a place where as one in a hundred, they have lost all individuality. No one else at my work does that.

I can write, publish, and sell my own book. This is the first time anyone in my family has done that.

....

*Interlude*

Forgive me for stopping in what feels like the middle of a train of thought, but let me explain. As I was telling Leigh tonight via Skype chat, I don't always know a lot about myself. I don't know if I'm quiet or loud, thoughtful or inconsiderate, patient or impatient. Most aspects of personality and character, especially when it comes to myself, completely evade me. This holds true for others, too… I couldn't tell you much about Leigh, either, other than the fact that she's Leigh and I don't want her any differently. But outstanding qualities and characteristics? Uh…

I'd like to add to this list that I have this outstanding character quality or that fruit of the Spirit, but the fact of the matter is, I don't rightly know what I am or what I have. The note to self has been made to work on figuring that out.

….

So I pick up where I left off. In Romans 12, Paul says that we are all part of Christ's body (which leads me to wonder if I'm a toe, or an eye, or a liver, but then I might be thinking too literally). Elsewhere, he questions us thusly: wouldn't it be ridiculous for the toe to fuss that it's not a hand, or the heart to complain that it's not the stomach? *I don't want to be kind, talkative, social, and a good singer… why can't I be like her, instead?*

Isn't that exactly what I'm doing in all my fussing? *I don't want to be autistic, a writer, a blogger, and a cat-lover… why can't I be like Mom/Sister/Leigh, instead?*

I can't have what they have for a simple reason: I have what I have, and that is no less wonderful, providential, and intentional.

It is just thus for you, and you, and you. *You* have a purpose that *only you* can fulfill. You were perfectly created with just the gifts, talents, and abilities to fulfill that purpose. God ordained it before time began… when it comes to your purpose, you cannot fail.

Isn't that a comforting thought? Let me say it again: *You can't fail to fulfill your purpose in life.* You don't even have to know what it is in order to accomplish it! Oh, sure, you might end up doing a lot more good along the way if you sort of take inventory of your qualities and capitalize on the best ones, but you can't fail to bring to fruition the very reason that God created you.

So rest easy, my friend. Take heart in the part of the body in which you reside; we would not be a complete body without you. You are not more or less than the toe, the hand, the heart, or the liver. You are *you*.

*So let's just go ahead and be what we were made to be.*

Ready?

Go.

So many people look at autism as solely a disability, when for many people, it is a combination of incredible gifts and surprising deficits. It's important to keep in mind that just because I do something differently than you do, it doesn't make me less able, less important, less human.

Autistic Speaks blog post
5 June, 2011
Big stuff

Well, I took my nighttime meds, so forgive me if I'm not so eloquent. I have "med brain" going on.

Today was so good. Mom took me to the zoo to watch the tiger cubs play. They were born in October, so they're quite big now but so very frisky and energetic! They take kitty baths, and have kitty noses, and expose kitty bellies. Big kitties! Mom is Mom, so she didn't hurry me up or even try to ruin it by talking to me while I watched them. I watched them for fifteen or twenty minutes on the way in, then another few minutes on the way out. As long as I wanted.

But something's been nagging at me… you see, someone online said that one of many reasons she wants to cure her children's autism is so that they can worship God freely.

So I've been thinking six ways to Sunday (or what's that expression? That's not quite right, but you know what I mean) about how I worship God.

First, I thought about all the ways most people worship Him.

Well, I don't usually sing in church (and when I do, well, I'm kind of a tenor, so it's quiet for sure!).

I can't listen to sermons for more than a few minutes without some major internal combustion going on.

I like to pray, but I'm lucky if I get three or four words out before I forget what I was talking about or even forget that I'm praying altogether.

As for reading the Bible, well... confession... and don't kill me... but it kind of bores me. I like to hear the stories how they tell them to the kids. Then I can pay attention.

So, my first conclusion is that I must not worship God, right?

You see, God made people in part so that we would worship Him. I am human. Therefore, I was created to worship. We can delineate "NTs" and "Aspies" and "auties" and what have you, but frankly, when it comes to certain things, those terms are meaningless. In fact, I'm not sure God even judges us with respect to neurological status, just like He doesn't judge us by our races or the languages that we speak. Just because you speak German and I speak English doesn't mean that we don't both worship. Or because you're Latina and I'm white, right? So why does it matter that I'm "an autie" and you're not? God doesn't see that. God created us ALL to honor and glorify Him.

So then I got to thinking some more.

You mostly talk; I mostly write. We both communicate.

You like to hug; I hate to be touched. We both share love.

You like dogs. I like cats. We both love animals. (Or, maybe you don't like them one bit, and that's okay too!)

So, maybe… just maybe… you worship by singing and reading and praying and whatnot, and I worship by…

Wait. Do I have your attention? How *does* someone with autism worship?

I can only tell you how I do, is the answer. I don't *know* how "people with autism" worship, not least because I am not "people" but just "Lydia." So what follows, as with anything I tell you, can only be certifiably true with respect to me, and only me.

I worship when I watch cats, because I totally revel in God's amazing ability to create them. Not just that He can, but that He *did*. That he thought them up and brought them into being out of nothing at all. That's cool.

I worship when I take a walk and totally marvel at everything, from what staff dubbed "a disease" growing on a tree, to the tadpole that just got his legs, to giggling uncontrollably at the ducks.

I worship in the light. No, not the *Light,* though I worship in him too… but the actual light. The way it comes through the stained glass windows in the sanctuary, the way my glasses make it spread out. And the way I see a complete rainbow surround every light that I look at.

I worship in the music, even though I don't sing. The harmonies, especially, just make everything right in my world.

I worship in the people. You would never, ever know it (you might not even think I notice, in fact), but I so feed off the joy in other people when they worship. I feel like I could simply explode with joy… but I don't think you'd notice a thing, not even a smile, because my face is probably too busy ticcing.

I worship when I type. God created me to type. It baffles me a bit, because as a very small child growing up in a non-Christian family, I questioned to myself whether it was possible that God creates people to do "unnatural" things, like driving (as opposed to horseback riding, which seems natural to me) or computers. The answer is, from personal experience, unequivocally yes. (As an aside, those are the sorts of things I wondered about as a preschooler...).

I worship in poetry. Now, I can't much understand other people's poetry, but the rhythms and the rhymes that I can create entirely capture me.

I worship in stimming... mostly, when I get really excited, I flap my hands and walk on my toes. But then, things like swinging and spinning in chairs and swimming make me excited too.

I worship when I create, whether it's words, stories, poems, necklaces, doll clothes... My Creator made the world and everything in it, and I am a reflection of Him; therefore, I too, love to create.

Oh, and here's a big one, and then I'll stop: I worship when I answer *every single question* that has *ever* been asked of me about ASD. Unless something crazy happens and I somehow can't keep up (which I don't foresee!), I will continue to do that for as long as I possibly can. Feed my sheep, right?

You sing. I listen to the music.

You read the Bible; I experience the world to learn about it.

You listen to sermons; I talk to parents.

You pray; I write.

We both worship.

I do not worship with limitations. I do not worship "unfreely." I am not held back because the music hurts my ears. In fact (I do not this to be the least been condescending; I just mean to point out what strikes me as odd when people say I have limitations), I certainly wonder how you worship at all when you're so busy rushing to get home that you don't stop to giggle at the ducks; when you're so occupied with singing that you don't see, and may never see even when I point them out, the lights; when you have so many things to discuss with God, that you forget how to just *be* with Him. To listen.

Me? Not free?

Think again.

Children with autism have services in school and often have private services (speech, occupational or physical therapy, counseling, psychiatrists, wraparound, etc), but parents are more or less on their own when it comes to making it through church. The following addresses the issue of how to help an autistic child to thrive within the church.

*How are autism and your faith interconnected?*

My faith and autism are the two most pervasive things in my life. I can draw parallels between them, such as the way they both affect everything I do and the way I view the world through glasses colored by both of them. They are both within me and can't be separated from me. If you take away my faith, or if you take away autism, there is no being left to survive.

Being autistic and a Christian raises some issues. Christianity is primarily based on a relationship between two beings, and my deficits in forming relationships are part of my autism diagnosis. I just don't "connect" very well. I can't say I find it easy or natural to connect with God, either, and I find my relationship with him waxing and waning in intensity. I suppose this is perfectly normal, or rather than it happens to all people and not just autistic ones. I try to keep in mind that God is the one person who will meet me wherever I am. I don't have to meet Him halfway or be anything I'm not; He'll come to me, however I am.

Religion in general also requires a fair amount of abstraction, and this really causes me to struggle. Everything from understanding that parables aren't meant to be taken literally to taking Communion to directives in the Bible that say to gouge out your eyes have, at some point, given me trouble. One thing I know about myself is that I don't generalize well, just like many people with autism. So, if I read a parable and someone reminds me not to take it literally, then next week I read another parable... I'll take it literally. Or if I'm told that the command to cut off your hand if it causes you to sin isn't literal, and then I read about gouging out eyes... I'm back to being literal. It's just not natural for me to think abstractly.

A college friend of mine once told me, and this is a rough paraphrase, that if God creates a person a certain way, then He won't hold it against the person if he can't fulfill certain commandments. For example, my friend's aunt had mild intellectual disability and could not read the Bible. Her point was that God would not punish her for this, as He created her perfectly and in His image. So, when I have trouble with looking outside myself, or when I can't sing at church, or when I have to take breaks during Bible study, I know that God doesn't hold that against me. He created me just the way He wanted me, and I was born with autism, so when my autism makes it hard for me to do what a "regular" Christian would do, He will understand.

This is not to say that I get a "get out of jail free" card with God, by any means. It does mean that I might have to do things a little differently. For example, God commands us to pray continually. Most people would understand this to mean "talk to God." But I don't pray out loud, and I don't even think in words. What I can do, though, is write to God, which does come naturally to me. God also tells us to worship Him, but worship often takes place in large groups during which I'm so overwhelmed and uncomfortable that I can't focus on the actual worship. So, I worship in my own way, in writing and nature and art and stimming. I don't learn much from sermons, but I can read books in which the characters exemplify Christian living and values.

The absolute most important concepts I have learned through my faith centralize around one concept. First, I'm not perfect, but He is. Then, He created me in His image, just the way He wants me to be, and there is no better me to do the job he has put before me. I can't do it myself, but the God in me can move mountains.

*How can I help my child to sit through religious services?*

I have a bit of a love-hate relationship with church. I like the idea of it, but actually going and listening to loud music and trying to process sermons and all the bright lights and all those people who try to say hi to me... it's a little much. Okay, to be honest, it's a lot much. As Christians, we are meant to fellowship; we autistics tend to be solitary creatures. How can this be rectified?

First, make church fun for your child. If he likes the singing, or the organ, or even going up and down the steps over and over, emphasize that. If there is nothing at church itself that stands out, bring something small that your child will love, such as a small toy, a favorite snack or drink, or a notebook of blank paper just for drawing at church. It's important for young children to form good memories at church.

Make sure your child's senses are in check. A weighted lap pad, a compression vest, or nubby seat cushion help to provide stabilization. If your child is a sensory seeker, make sure to bring something to chew on or stim with, and sit near the front for more input. If your child is a sensory avoider, sit in the back, and arm yourselves with noise-cancelling headphones or earplugs. (As a warning, though, earplugs tend to hurt after about 20 minutes, so the headphones are best.) If lights or motion are the problem, bring sunglasses or a hat, or even both. All children should take periodic breaks in order to get more sensory input or get away from the sensory input.

A Social Story or visual schedule that outlines exactly what will happen during church will help young children to stay calm, because they will know what to expect. Older children who are used to the routine of church but have trouble following the sermon might benefit from a fill-in-the-blank outline with the major points of the sermon. If your child goes to a program during the sermon, try asking the church's youth group if anyone would be willing to accompany him to the program and help him with transitions and following directions so that you can stay in the service.

Finally, start slow and celebrate every victory. If your child sits for one minute longer this week than he did last week, take it and build from there. If your child didn't sit at all but stayed in the sanctuary and not in the hallway, that is also a cause for celebration. It's all about baby steps.

If services prove simply too much for a child to handle at the present time, consider putting attendance on the back burner for a while. It's better to work with your child at home or in a small group than to force him to go to services and make him never want to go back. There have been periods of time that church has been more than my senses could take in, and so we take a break and go back when I am ready.

*How can I expose my child to religion at home?*

Children with autism learn differently than most children do. Therefore, we must teach them differently than we teach most children. Your child may not absorb much in children's religious programs, so you might want to supplement what he learns there each week while at home. Find out the schedule for what will be taught in the program, and work on the same material at home, with some modifications.

One important adjustment to make is that, while in class the story is read once, you might need to read the same story to your child every day for a week. Repetition is good for all children, but especially so for children with ASDs. It's also important to make everything you do with your child interactive. You don't have to sit and read the story out loud seven times, day after day. You can read it one day, draw it the next day, act it out a third day, color pictures about it the fourth day, fill-in-the-blanks as you read the fifth day, write a song about it the sixth day, and the seventh day would be class time.

Another consideration is that children with autism are very literal. Rather than reading them parables or commandments to "cut off your hand if it causes you to sin," try explaining to the child what the words actually mean. It's confusing to read words that mean something else, and you run the risk of your child taking the words completely literally. Now, here I am writing this, trying to give an example, and I can honestly say that I don't see any other way to take the cut off your hand commandment except literally! I'm sure it means something else, but I don't know what.

For children for whom receptive language is a struggle, use songs and pictures. I've mentioned before that some children who don't understand language very well can understand it much better when it's sung. This is a good opportunity to use this strategy. You might come up with pictures (Google is your friend!) for the main concepts and characters in the story you're teaching that week and use a magnetic or felt board to illustrate the stories.

One of the most important ways to teach children (again, all children, but especially those of the autistic variety) is to involve them. Don't teach them to serve others without actually taking them out to serve. When you teach them to pray, pray with them in the way they pray best (writing, art, dance, movement, any of the ways of communicating I discussed earlier). When you tell them to love God, give them examples of what that looks like and then point out when you or the child actually does one of them. Lead by example, and learn by doing.

You'll hear a lot of things about autism. You'll hear that autism is a terrible, evil thing that steals children from their parents, ruins marriages, and other horrible things. I would argue that every person with autism, by the very fact that they are people, have something to offer the world. You'll hear that autistics are simply "quirky geniuses" and that we'd be fine if allowed to form an autistic society. I must say, I don't buy that, because if everyone were autistic, who would be there to take care of us all? A solely autistic society might work for the mildest among us, but where does that leave the rest of us? So, that model doesn't fit for me either.

I see autism, for me, as a disorder that leads to amazing strengths and surprising deficits. As I think is clear from my writing at this point, at times I take major issue with autism and some of its "friends" (GI issues, anxiety, depression, sensory issues, etc), but the actual triad of impairments, the autism itself, brings so much good along with the bad. If it makes me who I am, I wouldn't trade it. Sure, I'd like life to be easier, but I think we would all like that. This is the life God saw fit to give me. He created me in His image. He created me to love cats, to sew, and to write…to be happy, and healthy, and smart… and he created me to be autistic. Who am I to argue with that?

## Afterward

Four years ago, I was facing the crisis of my life thus far and had little hope for the future. Two years ago, I was aimless and struggling to communicate. One year ago, I was facing a series of physical illnesses that would change life, as I knew it, forever.

Today, I'm halfway through my first semester of grad school, pulling an A average, and I'm putting in job applications... just to hold me over until I can get a position as a professor and fulfill my dream, which is to make unsuspecting freshman fall hard for writing. I also want to mentor kids and teens on the spectrum. I *know* what lost, confused, unwanted, uncertain, and unhappy feels like. I want to pass on the courage and confidence I've gained, the hard way, to kids who will need it. Because everybody needs it, but I think kids with autism might need it most of all. This world will never (okay, rarely) work in our favor, but that doesn't mean we can't make it, and stay true to ourselves in the process.